"I've been following Carissa on social media for years and have always been a huge fan. Every recipe I've made from the book so far has been seriously SO good! From the Spicy Rosé Spritz, to the Seared Ahi Tuna, to the Crunchy Shrimp Roll Bowl, I can't wait to make it all again . . . and again, and again. Carissa's book will be a kitchen staple for me!"

—**Hunter King,** actress

"Carissa has truly nailed it with *Seriously, So Good.* The bright colors, bold flavors, and variety of wholesome ingredients she uses in her recipes will surely bring more life into your everyday cooking!"

—**Rachael DeVaux,** *New York Times* bestselling author of *Rachael's Good Eats*

"Everything about Carissa's book makes you feel like you invited your best gal pal Brocc over to cook alongside you in your own kitchen—gossiping, giggling, and celebrating with every step. With seriously delicious chapters like 'Restaurant Remakes,' 'Soup Queen,' and 'Piece of Cake,' I have a feeling she may be moving in permanently!"

—**Dan Pelosi,** *New York Times* bestselling author of *Let's Eat: 101 Recipes to Fill Your Heart and Home*

"Cariss staple in my kitchen. The amount of delicious, simple, *real-food* recipes that she's packed into one book is incredible, plus she includes lists to make sure your pantry is strategically stocked. If you like fresh, nutritious, and satisfying meals, this book is for you."

—**Lauryn Bosstick,** The Skinny Confidential

"It's one thing to have a cookbook full of craveable, flavor-driven recipes that don't require twelve pots and five components. It's another to have a cookbook that feels like you're cooking alongside your fun (and funniest) friend. In *Seriously, So Good,* Carissa effortlessly delivers both."

—**Sarah Fennel,** author of *Sweet Tooth*

Seriously, So Good

Seriously, So Good

Simple Recipes for a Balanced Life

Carissa Stanton

Photography by Alanna Hale

SIMON
ELEMENT

New York London Toronto Sydney New Delhi

SIMON ELEMENT

An Imprint of Simon & Schuster, LLC
1230 Avenue of the Americas
New York, NY 10020

First Simon Element hardcover edition April 2024

SIMON ELEMENT is a trademark of Simon & Schuster, LLC

Simon & Schuster: Celebrating 100 Years of Publishing in 2024

For information about special discounts for bulk purchases, please
contact Simon & Schuster Special Sales at 1-866-506-1949 or
business@simonandschuster.com.

The Simon & Schuster Speakers Bureau can bring authors to
your live event. For more information or to book an event, contact
the Simon & Schuster Speakers Bureau at 1-866-248-3049
or visit our website at www.simonspeakers.com.

Food Stylist: Laura Kinsey Dolph

Prop Stylist: Jaclyn Kershek

Assistant Food Stylist: Danielle Marin

Assistant Prop Stylist: Hina Mistry

Designer: Mia Johnson

Manufactured in the United States of America

3 5 7 9 10 8 6 4

Library of Congress Cataloging-in-Publication Data
has been applied for.

ISBN 978-1-6680-2072-2
ISBN 978-1-6680-2073-9 (ebook)

To the Broccolinis

Contents

Acknowledgments

First and foremost, none of this would be possible without my incredible community, the Broccolinis. You all have given me the rare opportunity to have hundreds of thousands of cheerleaders that got me through the rejection, late nights, and countless hours of dishes. The thought of this book in your hands has truly gotten me through the hardest moments, and I cannot even begin to express my gratitude for this amazing community. You mean the world to me!

Mom: You have always been so confident in me and given me the courage to be something great. You have taught me so much about cooking from a young age, but more importantly, you have taught me the importance of enjoying what I make. You instilled in me that cooking and creating delicious food means memories, quality time with friends and family, and a connection to the ones we love, whether they're with us or watching down. You have inspired so many recipes in this book, many of which we developed in the kitchen together, and I feel so incredibly lucky to have those memories in this book forever.

Dad: Your never-ending support and tough love have given me the confidence and thick skin I needed to get through making this book. I could not have asked for better parents, and I feel endlessly grateful to be your daughter. Your love, guidance, and, of course, grilling tips have made this book possible, and I hope you know how much I love and appreciate you always being there for me.

Amanda, my best friend and sister: You have been my biggest fan since literally day one. I am so lucky to have a built-in best friend who will always be there cheering me on, along with my forever honest taste testers Kinsley and Charlie. From testing out recipes to always giving me an honest opinion, you have played such an important role in the creation of this book, and I am so incredibly grateful for you.

Corey, my sweet boyfriend: We fell in love in the midst of developing this book, and you immediately did everything you could do to support me, from doing countless hours of dishes without one complaint and helping me be patient and present throughout this whole process, to even helping me brush my teeth without having to get out of bed during my longest of days. You have been the most selfless and caring partner, and I am so grateful for you and your love.

My one-in-a-million best friends: Where would I be without you all?! My sounding board, my recipe testers, my hype girls, my everything! To Cassandra, Tori, Katie, Brooke, Andrea, Rio, Karina, Shannon, Janne, Ashley, Aubrianna, Maari, Christina, Emily, Ria, Gina, Teal, Shane, Suzee, Hanna, and Valerie, thank you for being there for me from the start and listening to me talk about this book for years. We are the luckiest to have one another.

My Instagram friends–made-real friends: Alex Snodgrass, thank you for being my mentor and gearing me up for this wild process. To Olivia, Tayla, Tori, Katie, Cameron, Rachael, Lea, Hanna, Victoria, and Ella, just to name a few, you have been the best role models and support system a girl could ask for. Thank you for always inspiring me.

Ali Wald, my manager at DBA: Thank you for helping make my dream a reality. You have been my right-hand woman throughout this entire journey, and I am so thankful to have such an incredibly hard worker on my team. This is just the beginning!

Andrea Barzvi, my literary agent at Empire Literary: I am so lucky to have such an incredible advocate for this book. You have gone above and beyond to make this book a success and having you behind me every step of the way has meant the world to me. Thank you for believing in me and putting your force behind my vision.

Lauren Deen: I think we both know this book would not be what it is without you. Not only did you make and test every single recipe in this book (!!!), you truly understood my vision and embodied my voice and personality throughout the whole book. You showed me what it takes to be a cookbook author, and whether I was ready for it or not, I am so thankful you were there for me throughout it all. I'm still in awe about how much work we accomplished together. We deserve endless Texas Sheet Cake for eternity.

Alanna Hale, my incredibly talented photographer: Not only did you take my exact vision and make it come to life, you made it so fun every step of the way! Without you, I would be doing my terrible fake smile in every photo instead of genuinely cracking up about something wild that you said. I am endlessly grateful for you and will never be able to listen to "2 Phones" without thinking of you.

Laura Kinsey, my food stylist: You are such a one-of-a-kind human, and I am already looking forward to working with you again just so we can spend more time together. I still cannot believe you made every single recipe in this book look (and taste) so beautiful while staying true to my down-to-earth style. And thank you to your wonderful assistant, Danielle, who was beyond a joy to work with as well. You both are so incredible!

Jaclyn Kershek, my prop stylist: Thank you for sliding into my DMs at the perfect time and asking if you could be my prop stylist. I am so honored to have your brilliant touch throughout this book. I will say I didn't really know what your job entailed at that time, but boy was I surprised at how your expertise shaped the way this book looks and feels. Thank you for giving this book your all.

Justin Schwartz, my editor at Simon & Schuster: Thank you for believing in me as a first-time author and giving me the freedom to create something I am so proud of. Having an editor whose passion for food rivals my own is such an honor. In addition, a huge thank-you to the entire team at Simon Element, including Elizabeth Breeden and Jessica Preeg, who have done a magnificent job of promoting this book.

Mia Johnson, book designer: Thank you for embodying my vision and creating such a visually stunning book. I have always had an idea of what my first cookbook would look like, and you did a dazzling job at bringing it to life.

Izzy: Thank you for helping me bring this book to life. You were there straight from the very beginning with designing the book proposal, to being there for me in every capacity during the photo shoot. You were such a light, and I will never forget you always making everyone laugh. I know you're looking down and are so proud of what we accomplished together. I feel so lucky to have some of your one-of-a-kind energy encapsulated in this book forever.

I am endlessly grateful for everyone who helped me with this book! I feel like I could go on forever naming each individual person who was a part of this journey. I could not have done it without you all so thank you for being a part of this wild journey. We did it!!

INTRODUCTION

I don't want to just give you a book full of recipes.

I want to show you just how fun cooking can be.

I learned how to cook from anyone who would teach me—family, friends, and people whose cooking made me come back for seconds. None of them were trained chefs but that didn't matter. They excited and inspired me just the same, helped give me the freedom and confidence to try things in the kitchen, and helped me build up my culinary game. But back in 2017, when I became "Brocc" and first started posting my recipes to Instagram and my blog, I have to admit I felt like a bit of an imposter for a while because I never went to culinary school—and had never even watched a cooking video on YouTube if I'm being honest. I was convinced that my lack of training was my biggest weakness. It took me a long time to realize that was actually my greatest strength. I'm not trying to follow someone else's rules, always cooking with another person's voice in my head. Because it's just me out here! And that's why I think my cooking is accessible, simple, and achievable. I don't use fancy techniques or rely on ingredients you've never heard of. It's just me and my likes, dislikes, and instincts. Easy to follow and simple to make. Just turn to one of my recipes and jump in. It'll be fun, I promise.

Cooking can be relaxing and really satisfying and it's so important for your quality of life. But first, we have to lose the expectations and pressure. I don't want you to stress about cooking dinner, or cooking for other people, or any of it. So let's keep it that way. My goal with this book is to help you find the joy in cooking, for any occasion, with simple, seriously good food.

Most of the recipes in this book take less than an hour to prepare, and there's a whole chapter of recipes that take thirty minutes or less. Dishes made up of things you probably already have in your fridge or pantry . . . or should. (And if you don't, I've got lists to help you get organized and not overwhelmed.) Dips, sauces, dressings, and marinades that are delicious on a million other things. Apps, soups, mains, sides, desserts, and cocktails of course. Plus, each recipe is filled with helpful info, tips, shortcuts, and swaps— easy ways to modify the dish for both your personal taste, diet, or food sensitivities. And also, hopefully, to get you excited to get in the kitchen. It's all there, in these one hundred recipes. The only thing left for you to do is give it a try. I'm here for you.

My hope is that these dishes, drinks, and treats will bring you comfort and help you connect and hang out with friends.

A Little Something About Me

While my passport says Carissa, I'll also answer to Brocc. No, I'm not obsessed with broccoli, though it's a damn good veg. I earned the nickname "Brocc Your Body" from my friends because I love to cook and to move. I'm a California native who grew up at the beach surrounded by a close family. I studied kinesiology with an emphasis on fitness, health, and nutrition at San Diego State University. Though passionate about my studies, after graduating I struggled to find a great job in my field, working in real estate full-time and grabbing a side hustle as a server at night to help support myself. Neither job was what you would call fulfilling for me personally. I felt fairly stuck, especially on the creative front. The one thing I really looked forward to were my weekly Girls' Night dinner parties with my friends, a place where I could channel my creativity and energy.

I loved cooking for our GN hangouts, and the dishes I created were such a hit that my friends would always ask me for the recipes. Instead of texting them, I started to post them to my personal Instagram and then decided the food from Girls' Night deserved its very own page. So along with my nickname, my friends thought it would be hilarious to name the page Brocc Your Body after Justin Timberlake's "Rock Your Body," and I started posting away to the new Brocc IG as a hobby. To my surprise, Brocc soon exploded into an Instagram and social media success, allowing me to leave my real estate job and waitressing gig behind and concentrate on Brocc as a full-time career in food and wellness. While at first I posted mostly about food and friends, I soon tackled more serious subjects and began sharing everything

from my struggles with anxiety and panic disorder to a major breakup, to my dating life, to learning to love myself, and just the ins and outs of my everyday life. There's really nothing that's off-limits over here, and it will always stay that way!

What started as a space for my friends took off and became an amazing full-time job with a fantastic online community of hundreds of thousands of incredible people. So yes, I'll happily answer to Brocc, especially when it comes to questions from my beloved followers, whom I call my Broccolinis.

I'm so excited to share all that I've learned over the last six years while I spent my days (and my nights) cooking, blogging, posting, DMing, and connecting with my audience. I love the idea of having it all in a book that you can hold in your hand. A book on your shelf that you can turn to again and again for ideas, leafing through for inspiration and solutions that feed you. My hope is that these dishes, drinks, and treats will bring you comfort and help you connect and hang out with friends. And do it in any way that suits you—a relaxing low-key meal, a fancy dinner meant to impress, or anything in between—but mostly to reduce your stress and improve your life.

My goal is to inspire you to cook something almost daily (but I totally get it if that isn't your thing—I'll settle for once a week) and to have this book be your kitchen confidante and companion. I also hope these pages will give you a taste of the SoCal life I love so much—from my affordable homemade take on the fabulous salad found at La Scala (aka my Famous Beverly Hills Chopped Salad, page 125) to the feasts I throw around my backyard firepit, and even my sister Amanda's favorite cocktail, a Blackberry Mexican Mule (page 231).

Finding Balance

I believe in a healthy ratio of eating foods that nourish our bodies and foods that feed our souls. It's the way I intuitively eat every single day, but how did I get here? What works for me is my approach, which is this: All foods have a place in a healthy diet.

I don't follow or promote a specific diet—that's not what this book is about. It reflects my basic philosophy to remove the anxiety around food and to feel good about what I'm cooking and eating, making smart choices without depriving myself of delicious carbs or a splash of cream here and there. Tuning in to my body and paying close attention to how I feel after I eat have given me the freedom and flexibility to eat whatever I want, whenever I want. I know that eating lots of whole foods, like vegetables and lean proteins, gives me energy to keep up with my active lifestyle and makes me feel amazing, which is why I have mastered the art of making healthy food taste incredible. During the week I try to eat to feel my best—heavier on the veggies and those lean proteins—and on the weekends (or whenever the occasion calls for it) is when I'm more likely to be cooking up richer, more decadent dishes and stirring up cocktails with my friends.

You may notice that none of these recipes are geared toward any specific lifestyle or diet. They're not Whole30, keto, or all gluten-free, etc. Those diets are great if they work for you. Many of the recipes in the book will work for those diets or are adaptable to be gluten-free and dairy-free, which I share in the headnotes, along with any adjustments needed to make them just as delicious. I'm here to help.

So, when I have a busy week and I need to be on my A game, I'm cooking from the Feel Good Food chapter, like Turmeric Ginger Grain Bowls with Lemon-Tahini Sauce (page 111). When I'm finished with that busy week and I'm ready for the weekend, I'm getting cozy with a cheesy carb-heavy meal like Prosciutto and Parmesan Tagliatelle (page 129), because it feeds my soul and makes me so happy. When Sunday rolls around and I'm craving fast food, you can bet I am making a "Fried" Chicken Sandwich with Special Sauce (page 132), because it hits all the flavors I love but it's not deep-fried, so I know I'll be feeling great to start off my week on Monday. It's all about paying close attention to what your body is telling you.

Maybe gluten gives you a headache, or maybe pasta gives you tons of fuel . . . I can't tell you how food is going to make you feel because we are all unique, including the way our individual bodies process food. That's what makes life so fun! So instead of trying to fit into your high school jeans by cutting out carbs, let's toss the jeans and start boiling some water to make pasta, because life is about celebrating our changing bodies throughout our lifetime and enjoying our favorite foods along the way. Health isn't just about being able to run a marathon or eating "clean," it's about living your life to the fullest. For me, that involves vegetables *and* cheese.

ABOUT
THIS BOOK

I want you to have everything you need to make your cooking experience seamless, so I've included it up front in the book. Everything in this section leads you to the items every well-stocked kitchen needs, and I'll show you examples that are kind on both your counter space and your wallet.

It starts with the Grocery Run (page 11). These are foolproof tips for stocking your kitchen, a map to my forever shopping list, and a strategy for stocking your fridge, pantry, and freezer with items that you will use over and over. I'm not giving you recipes that rely on random spices or exotic, overpriced, or hard-to-find items that will collect dust in the graveyard section at the back of your pantry. These are things you'll use so often that you'll have them on auto-replenish!

Then there's the Kitchen Essentials (page 23) section, which will help you get your gear on—and finally organize those cluttered kitchen drawers. A properly outfitted kitchen makes your life easier and gets you back to your guests quicker, so no bulky one-use gadgets allowed! I've come up with a tightly edited list of must-have items that will help you slice and dice your way through these recipes with ease.

I've also got you covered with some Quick Tips (page 31), a collection of "suggestions"—I hate rules, but I promise if you follow them you'll be off to the best start on this kitchen adventure. Think of it as the quick-start guide you consult when you get your new phone. Oh, and to pull it all together I threw in a play-list, because what's cooking without a soundtrack? Scan the QR code below, or search "Seriously, So Good" on Spotify to listen.

About
the Recipes

These recipes are the real deal. I'm sharing what I actually eat and cook every day. It's what's truly happening, what my day is all about, not invented for Instagram. Sometimes it's craveable, quick, and clever, like Sheet Pan Gnocchi with Burst Cherry Tomatoes and Pesto (page 72) that's ready in under thirty minutes. Sometimes it's a dish thrown together entirely from a run to Trader Joe's, or better yet what's already in my pantry. These are recipes for real life that you will be making on repeat.

Each of these one hundred recipes is really special to me. Some are longtime fan favorites from my blog and Instagram, but the majority are brand-new. You will be obsessed with these easy and versatile recipes, because they're packed with flavor but don't call for a zillion steps or last-minute trips to a specialty store. You'll know where to find every ingredient and you won't be left with half a package of some random ingredient to kick around in your pantry for a year before you finally toss it. If you want exciting, flexible dishes that won't keep you chained to the stove—time better spent hanging out with your guests and sipping a fun cocktail—you're in the right place. If you want healthier versions of familiar comfort food favorites to share, with the occasional indulgence, then I think we should become friends (seriously, DM me on Instagram). These recipes don't claim to be something they're not, and I feel like they mirror our lives today: honest, fresh in flavor, bold in attitude, and, face it, a bit messy sometimes. And that's okay! It's all about embracing the real.

The recipes are organized into eight chapters:

Apps, Always: My favorite way to eat always—small bites, starters, small plates

Dinner in 30: Tasty time-crunch meals

Feel Good Food: Healthy, eat-the-rainbow food guaranteed to brighten your mood—things that are "good" for you but aren't diet food

Restaurant Remakes: A mix of my better-for-you takes on takeout with swaps that "health-up" heavier dishes and the secret to re-creating other fave restaurant dishes at home

Major Mains: Big-deal dishes guaranteed to impress, yet they won't overwhelm you

Soup Queen: Because that's the *other* name I will answer to!—and because these soups are really good

Cheers to That: Cocktails in every form, for every moment!—straight up, as slushies or spritzes, or by the icy pitcher

Piece of Cake: A variety of delish desserts that don't require pastry chef skills

That's the road map to the book! One hundred delicious stops ahead for great food that's simple, not stressful, good for you, fulfilling, satisfying, and (I promise) that all taste, seriously, so good. I'm here for you and I can't wait for you to start cooking!

GROCERY RUN

Consider this part the life coach/pantry makeover section, if you will. This is not just what you need and why you need it, but also some surprising ways to use pantry items and my desert island list of faves. This will save you endless trips to the grocery store, as often you'll be able to throw together a meal with what you have on hand. What a thrill!

Baking

- ☐ Baking Powder
- ☐ Baking Soda
- ☐ Chocolate Chips:
  - ☐ Bittersweet
  - ☐ Semisweet
- ☐ Flours:
  - ☐ All-purpose flour
  - ☐ 1:1 gluten-free all-purpose flour such as Bob's Red Mill or Cup4Cup's Multipurpose
  - ☐ Almond flour
  - ☐ Coconut flour
- ☐ Tapioca flour/starch (tapioca is great if you are nut-free)
- ☐ Sweeteners:
  - ☐ Coconut sugar
  - ☐ Light brown sugar
  - ☐ Honey
  - ☐ Maple syrup
  - ☐ White granulated sugar
  - ☐ Powdered sugar

Pantry

- [ ] Beans:
  - [ ] Canned:
    - [ ] Black beans (regular and refried)
    - [ ] Chickpeas
    - [ ] Great Northern
  - [ ] Dried:
    - [ ] Split peas
- [ ] Bread Crumbs:
  - [ ] Panko bread crumbs (aka Japanese style)
  - [ ] Italian bread crumbs
- [ ] Breads:
  - [ ] English muffins
  - [ ] Fresh sourdough bread
- [ ] Tortillas:
  - [ ] Spinach
  - [ ] Whole wheat
  - [ ] Almond flour such as Siete Foods brand
- [ ] Broths:
  - [ ] Shelf-stable cartons of beef, chicken, and vegetable
  - [ ] Better Than Bouillon jars of beef, chicken, and vegetable
- [ ] Canned Tomatoes:
  - [ ] San Marzano (28-ounce) whole, peeled
  - [ ] San Marzano (28-ounce) crushed
  - [ ] Diced tomatoes
  - [ ] Fire-roasted tomatoes with green chiles

- [ ] Coconut Milk:
  - [ ] Full-fat (my preference) or "lite"
- [ ] Condiments and Sauces:
  - [ ] Chipotles in adobo sauce
  - [ ] Crushed Calabrian chile peppers such as Tutto Calabria brand
  - [ ] Hot sauces such as Cholula, Crystal, and sriracha
  - [ ] Ketchup
  - [ ] Mayonnaise, regular and Asian Kewpie brand
  - [ ] Mustard, Dijon and yellow
  - [ ] Reduced-sodium soy sauce or tamari
  - [ ] Sun-dried tomatoes in oil
  - [ ] Tahini
  - [ ] Thai green curry paste
  - [ ] Worcestershire sauce
- [ ] Grains:
  - [ ] Rice:
    - [ ] Jasmine rice
    - [ ] Short-grain brown rice
    - [ ] Sushi rice
  - [ ] Quinoa
- [ ] Nuts and Seeds:
  - [ ] Almonds, roasted and salted
  - [ ] Cashews, roasted and salted
  - [ ] Macadamias, roasted and salted
  - [ ] Pistachios, roasted, salted, and shelled

- [ ] Pumpkin seeds, shelled and unsalted
- [ ] Sunflower seeds, shelled and unsalted
- [ ] Walnuts, raw and unsalted
- [ ] Oils:
  - [ ] Avocado oil
  - [ ] Extra-virgin olive oil (EVOO)
  - [ ] Toasted sesame oil
- [ ] Pasta (Dried):
  - [ ] Orzo
  - [ ] Rigatoni
  - [ ] Shells
  - [ ] Spaghetti
  - [ ] Couscous: North African (smaller), Israeli, or pearl
- [ ] Pasta sauce such as Rao's brand
- [ ] Salt and Pepper:
  - [ ] Kosher salt such as Diamond Crystal
  - [ ] Flaky sea salt such as Maldon
  - [ ] Tellicherry peppercorns
- [ ] Dried Spices and Herbs:
  - [ ] Bay leaves
  - [ ] Cajun seasoning
  - [ ] Cayenne pepper
  - [ ] Chili powder
  - [ ] Cinnamon, ground
  - [ ] Coriander, ground
  - [ ] Crushed red chile flakes
  - [ ] Cumin, ground
  - [ ] Curry powder, mild or yellow

- [ ] Dill, dried
- [ ] Garam masala
- [ ] Garlic powder
- [ ] Ginger, ground
- [ ] Italian seasoning
- [ ] Mustard powder
- [ ] Onion powder
- [ ] Oregano, dried
- [ ] Parsley, dried
- [ ] Smoked Spanish paprika
- [ ] Sumac
- [ ] Sweet paprika
- [ ] Taco Seasoning (see page 97)
- [ ] Turmeric, ground
- [ ] Vinegar:
  - [ ] Apple cider vinegar
  - [ ] Balsamic vinegar
  - [ ] Balsamic glaze
  - [ ] Distilled white vinegar
  - [ ] Red wine vinegar
  - [ ] Rice vinegar, unseasoned

Perishables

- [ ] Citrus:
  - [ ] Lemons
  - [ ] Limes
- [ ] Dairy and Subs:
  - [ ] Butter, unsalted and grass-fed
  - [ ] Cheese:
    - [ ] Cheddar
    - [ ] Cream cheese
    - [ ] Feta

- [ ] Gruyère
- [ ] Mozzarella
- [ ] Parmesan, grated
- [ ] Parmigiano-Reggiano hunk
- [ ] Shredded Mexican blend
- [ ] Spanish Manchego
- [ ] Greek yogurt: whole-milk, plain
- [ ] Milk:
  - [ ] Almond such as Three Trees brand
  - [ ] Half-and-half
- [ ] Heavy cream
- [ ] Vegetables:
- [ ] Greens:
  - [ ] Baby spinach
  - [ ] Little Gem
  - [ ] Mixed greens
  - [ ] Romaine
- [ ] Fresh herbs:
  - [ ] Basil
  - [ ] Cilantro
  - [ ] Dill
  - [ ] Mint
  - [ ] Parsley
  - [ ] Oregano
  - [ ] Rosemary
  - [ ] Sage
  - [ ] Thyme
- [ ] Garlic
- [ ] Onions, yellow and red
- [ ] Shallots

Freezer

- [ ] Frozen Fruit:
  - [ ] Berries
  - [ ] Organic mixed fruit such as Trader Joe's or Whole Foods
- [ ] Frozen Vegetables:
  - [ ] Frozen ginger such as Trader Joe's ginger cubes
- [ ] Meat:
  - [ ] Chicken breasts, boneless and skinless
  - [ ] Chicken thighs, boneless and skinless
  - [ ] Chicken sausages
  - [ ] Ground beef
  - [ ] Ground turkey
  - [ ] Ground lamb
  - [ ] Pork chops
  - [ ] Steaks such as flank, rib-eye, or sirloin
- [ ] Shrimp, large and peeled
- [ ] Tequila such as Casamigos Blanco

I like to plan my meals, my menus, and my get-togethers to be as efficient as possible—not because I'm a control freak, but frankly because I'm a bit lazy and want to save my energy for my family, friends, or guests. That's why I designed my recipes to deliver big flavor while not overwhelming you with ingredients. But to accomplish that I learned you have to be strategic with your shopping and pantry organization. I'm so excited about this section because once you have this foundation and are familiar with your go-to ingredients, cooking any meal will just become second nature. Your life is about to become so much easier.

I don't believe in hunting down obscure ingredients or making trips to three different stores to get dinner on the table. I also can't bear buying ingredients you'll use for only one recipe—double duty or nothing! It's just not realistic and it's not the Brocc way! I consider your fridge and the freezer an extended pantry and arsenal to help you get through busy weeks, inspire you for bigger cooking projects, and for last-minute guests. By following my pantry, fridge, and freezer suggestions, you'll have what you need within reach and be ready for anything—a last-minute brunch, Sunday supper with the family, or even an unexpected romantic date night—without stressing out about it.

Pantry

Here are my must-haves—in alphabetical, not favorite, order!

Baking: In my pantry you'll always find some baking powder, baking soda, vanilla extract (always real vanilla, never artificial! It's worth spending a bit more, and Costco is a good place to get it), and of course, chocolate chips. I'm a fan of both bittersweet and semisweet chocolates, but get whatever you like. And here are my other baking essentials . . .

Flours: You're nowhere without a bag of all-purpose flour on hand for baking, thickening sauces, breading, etc. If you're gluten-free, you can always swap it for a 1:1 gluten-free all-purpose flour, like the one from Bob's Red Mill, or Cup4Cup's Multipurpose Flour. We are now living in the new world of alternative flours, so others I reach for often are coconut flour, almond flour, and tapioca flour (also known as tapioca starch), which is a great way to get a nice crispy coating on chicken, fish, etc.—all of these are great gluten-free choices. Coconut and almond flours add a bit of extra flavor, while tapioca is great if you are nut-free.

Sweeteners: My go-to sweeteners are honey and maple syrup for everything from my morning coffee to adding a touch of sweetness to salad dressing or sauces. But that doesn't mean I'm a stranger to regular granulated white sugar and brown sugar, especially when it comes to baking. Coconut sugar makes a great swap for regular white or brown sugar if you're looking for something a bit cleaner. It has a more caramelly flavor, closer to brown sugar.

Beans: I always have cans of black beans (regular and refried), chickpeas, and Great Northern beans in my pantry. Several recipes in this book use these and it's always so helpful to have them on hand. From salads to grain bowls to enchiladas to soups, the list is long and gratifying. Plus, they've got a ton of fiber and are a great vegan source of protein! Perfect for when I'm too lazy to cook meat. Note: I said cans, but dried beans are great, too—and often cheaper—but remember they require extra time to prep and soak, and honestly, I don't bother, but I applaud you.

Bread and tortillas: I usually have either fresh sourdough bread or English muffins on hand for my breakfasts or for a quick sandwich. I also love having whole wheat or spinach tortillas for wraps, like my Mediterranean-Style Tuna Wrap (page 130). You will also find me mentioning Siete Foods brand almond flour tortillas quite frequently throughout the book, which I use in my Crispy Mushroom Tacos (page 97) and Bean and Cheese Enchiladas (page 89). I love this brand because they make flavorful grain-free tortillas with clean ingredients.

Bread crumbs: Panko bread crumbs (aka Japanese style) are extra crispy and make quite a few cameos in this book. I toast them up to add crunch to a dish or to top a salad, or I use them as breading, like with my crispy Coconut Fish Tacos with Mango Salsa (page 79). I occasionally use traditional bread crumbs as well, like in my mom's Spinach and Cheddar–Stuffed Meatloaf with Extra Sauce (page 184).

Broths: You should have a few cartons of shelf-stable chicken and vegetable broth in your pantry at all times, so you can whip up a soup with leftover chicken and vegetables or make a quick pan sauce (see Date Night Chicken in Creamy Mushroom Sauce, page 71). There's also a great product called Better Than Bouillon, which is stock in paste form—just add boiling water. Comes in every flavor imaginable: chicken, beef, and vegetable in a shelf-stable jar. I first discovered it at Costco and have been hooked since.

Canned tomatoes: I'm not big on canned vegetables—I'll go with fresh or even frozen before grabbing the can opener—but that's not the case with canned San Marzano tomatoes. They're delicious year-round and are sweeter and less acidic than most canned tomatoes. They're a real game changer in the kitchen: great in soups, sauces, or anytime fresh tomatoes aren't cutting it. Wondering what to do with that 28-ounce can is actually what inspired my Pantry Tomato Soup with Puff Pastry (page 210)!

Coconut milk: Perfect for creamy soups and curries. Plus, I've been known to use the last bits of a can in my smoothies instead of the usual yogurt or milk! You can go full-fat or "lite." I prefer full-fat because it makes things really creamy, but get one of each and decide for yourself. They definitely won't go to waste!

Condiments and sauces: Condiments and sauces can add that last little pop to any meal, but they're also the building blocks for so many other types of sauces, plus dressings and marinades. Besides the obvious trifecta of ketchup, mayonnaise, and mustard (you should always have yellow and Dijon on hand), I'll sometimes grab another, like an Asian sauce that catches my eye, because they'll keep well and always come in handy for a fridge-clean-out stir-fry. I'm not too specific about brands, but I can tell you I have been loving Kewpie mayo lately. It's a touch sweeter and they use an extra egg yolk, so it's richer and, in my opinion, just tastes better (buy it online or at a Japanese market). Jarred green curry paste is another lifesaver for quick stir-fries and vital for a quick Coconut Green Curry Shrimp (page 116), along with canned chipotles in adobo sauce to zing up a pot of chili and deliver smoky heat to One-Pot Chipotle Chicken and Rice (page 104).

Crushed Calabrian chile peppers: My must-have condiment to put on pasta, pizza, in salad dressing, on sandwiches, or anytime you need a little spice. I order the Tutto Calabria brand online.

Hot sauce: Essential, but not all hot sauces are the same! I keep a few different ones on hand for different uses. I love the slightly softer heat and sweetness of Cholula for most of my Mexican dishes, sriracha for Asian dishes (and eggs!), and Crystal for when I need something with a vinegar base.

Reduced-sodium soy sauce or tamari: A must for cooking any Asian dishes and stir-fries, also a regular ingredient in everything from marinades to salad dressings. It's the secret ingredient in my carne asada for the California Burrito Bowls (page 146), too.

Tahini: A fun name for ground-up sesame seeds. It's a great base for sauces, dressings, marinades, and, of course, for traditional chickpea hummus or my White Bean Hummus (page 62). You can find it at Trader Joe's or try one of my favorites at Whole Foods or order online from Seed and Mill, which I love to support because it's a small woman-owned business.

Worcestershire sauce: Great for adding a nice savory depth of flavor to sauces, soups, and dressing. And you can't make my Soupe à l'Oignon (page 194) without it!

Grains: As you can tell by reading my book, I eat rice a lot. I love it! Whether white or brown, it's often at the bottom of one of my bowls. I usually go for jasmine rice or short-grain brown rice, and sushi rice for Spicy Tuna Crispy Rice (page 144). You'll need high-protein nutty quinoa for the Turmeric Ginger Grain Bowls with Lemon-Tahini Sauce (page 111).

Nuts and seeds: Where would I be without my cashews, almonds, walnuts, pistachios, macadamias, and pumpkin and sunflower seeds? Dream it, and you can throw nuts or seeds into it: Elevate a simple salad with crunch and heft, great in stir-fries and as a snack whenever you need a quick boost. Is there anything they can't do? They can even transport you to Hawaii with the Hawaiian-Style Chicken Bowls with Pineapple and Macadamia Nut Slaw (page 94)!

Oils: The two oils I use 99 percent of the time are extra-virgin olive oil (EVOO) and avocado oil. Since avocado oil has a higher smoke point than olive oil (meaning it can take higher temperatures), it's great when you're pan searing and trying to get a nice crust on something. I use olive oil more for soups, stews, sauces, salad dressings, and finishing drizzles. When it comes to extra-virgin olive oil I'm reaching for the more mellow, lighter, floral oils over the peppery oils. I use toasted sesame oil to add a nutty Asian touch to dishes and stir-fries, such as Hibachi-Style Fried Rice with Ginger Sauce (page 126) and many dressings.

Pasta: Pasta is one of my favorite foods and a lifesaver when I find myself in a dinner pinch or I'm looking to use up any leftovers in my fridge at the end of the week. You can usually find my favorite shapes—rigatoni, shells, spaghetti, and orzo—in my pantry, but I think we can all agree fresh pasta reigns supreme if it's accessible to you. I also grew up on couscous, which is like teeny-tiny pasta that's delicious as the bed for a stew, in a salad, or as a side for my Meme's Chicken Tagine (page 173). Israeli or pearl couscous is larger than the North African version, and it rocks in salads and soups, too.

Pasta sauce: Look, I have all the respect in the world for homemade pasta sauce, I really do, and when I have the time I'll make it myself, but let's face it . . . I use a lot of jarred pasta sauce in my daily life. It's a convenient, cleanup-free choice, and if you spend a few bucks more on the good stuff, like Rao's, you can save yourself a ton of time with no real downside.

Salt and pepper: Salt is life! It balances your dishes, sauces, vinaigrettes, and salsas; it helps to deliver that perfect sear on your steak . . . it brings the magic to your kitchen.

Kosher salt: If there's one thing I learned from watching the Food Network, it was the importance of using kosher salt instead of regular table salt when cooking. This is for a few reasons: One, because the larger flakes are easier to feel when you're picking up a pinch, you tend not to oversalt things. And two, I find kosher salt definitely tastes cleaner, less bitter. Diamond Crystal is my go-to brand; I order in bulk online. Please note that if you use Morton brand kosher salt or regular fine-grain table salt, you should use half as much in the recipes because it's denser, and the teaspoon amounts will be saltier.

Flaky sea salt: It adds drama to a finishing presentation. Maldon is my go-to brand. I love the little pyramid shapes and the clean taste, and use it to finish everything from my Goat Cheese Crostini with Tomato Confit (page 50) to my Flourless Espresso Brownies (page 235). A little sprinkled over cut slices of rare steak? Heaven.

Black pepper: Freshly cracked always! I'm partial to Tellicherry peppercorns, which are pretty easy to find in your local supermarket.

Spices and herbs: Having the proper spices and dried herbs on hand will make your life so much easier, and your cooking more inspiring and exciting. Below you'll find every spice, spice blend, or herb needed to make all the recipes in this book. Taste them, experiment, use them generously, and have fun with them! These are ingredients you'll use again and again, I promise, not buy once and then stare at them for the rest of your life.

- ☐ Bay leaves
- ☐ Cajun seasoning
- ☐ Cayenne pepper
- ☐ Chili powder
- ☐ Cinnamon, ground
- ☐ Coriander, ground
- ☐ Crushed red chile flakes
- ☐ Cumin, ground
- ☐ Curry powder, mild or yellow
- ☐ Dill, dried
- ☐ Garam masala
- ☐ Garlic powder
- ☐ Ginger, ground
- ☐ Italian seasoning
- ☐ Mustard powder
- ☐ Onion powder
- ☐ Oregano, dried
- ☐ Parsley, dried
- ☐ Smoked Spanish paprika
- ☐ Sumac
- ☐ Sweet paprika
- ☐ Taco seasoning (You can find this in any supermarket, but I'm pretty proud of my recipe! After MUCH trial and error, I created my own blend. See page 97.)
- ☐ Turmeric, ground

Sun-dried tomatoes: I use the type that are packed in oil, and they are a must for throwing into pasta, sandwiches, and salads. They are also the secret to keeping my Sun-Dried Tomato and Feta Turkey Burgers with Jalapeño Tzatziki (page 115) extra juicy!

Vinegar: Vinegar is one of the most important pantry staples, essential for adding that much-needed touch of acidity to a dish, plus it lasts forever in your pantry so you don't need to worry about it going bad. Vinegars have totally different tastes based on what they're made from. I always have rich, sweet balsamic vinegar; brighter and sometimes fruitier or slightly bitter red wine vinegar; bracing distilled white vinegar; tart apple cider vinegar; and mellow, slightly sweet rice vinegar stocked. I also love a balsamic glaze, which is a reduced regular balsamic vinegar: thick, tart but sweet, and great as a topping on pasta, pizza, sandwiches, salads, and so on.

Fridge

Citrus: More often than not, a recipe can benefit from a squeeze of fresh lemon or lime. You will notice this trend in many of my recipes. It's a great, healthy way to bring some brightness to a dish and really balance out all the flavors. I can't list a recipe here because I think I used them in almost every recipe . . . Okay, maybe the one dessert that celebrates it the most is my No-Bake Key Lime Pie with Pretzel Crust (page 236).

Dairy and subs:

Butter (grass-fed): Growing up in the nineties, I feel like it was instilled in us that butter was the enemy in terms of health and wellness. Surprisingly, high-quality grass-fed butter has a ton of health benefits when eaten in moderation; plus, it is extremely delicious (you can't deny!). I am not afraid to cook with butter, although I definitely eat it a bit less frequently than I used to. Again, balance is key! All the recipes call for unsalted butter.

Cheese: When I first started my blog, I would describe my cooking as "healthy, but with cheese on top" (lol!), and although we've come a long way since then, I think there is still a lot of truth in it. I love adding cheese to my recipes because, well, who doesn't love cheese? There's great quality in the domestic parms you can find these days, but for certain recipes like the Prosciutto and Parmesan Tagliatelle (page 129) I always have a hunk of real Parmigiano-Reggiano ready to be grated or shaved where the exceptional fruity, nutty, real-deal flavor truly makes a difference. Feta is perfect for crumbling on top of salads, eggs, and any dish that needs a creamy, salty component. I stock goat cheese for dips like Bacon, Date, and Goat Cheese Dip (page 57), along with cheddar, cream cheese, mozzarella, and shredded Mexican blend—also for dips and for everything in between melted on pizzas, enchiladas, chiles, and dressing up scrambled eggs. Many of these cheeses freeze well, too (see Freezer section below)! You'll often find a snacking cheese like Spanish Manchego (just throw it together with some olives for my recipe for Marinated Olives and Manchego, page 41) or Gruyère for Soupe à l'Oignon (page 194).

Greek yogurt: Another one of my secret weapons. I use whole-milk Greek yogurt for everything from breakfast bowls to salad dressings to a more versatile substitute for sour cream, although there are times when you need the real deal like in my Hungarian Mushroom Soup (page 202). Greek yogurt adds tang and a creamy texture while also lending a boost of protein to dishes. It's a win-win! I prefer whole milk to lowfat for the full, rich flavor, but of course, choose what's best for you.

Milk: I am an almond milk girl through and through, especially when it comes to my morning iced latte or using it as a substitute for regular milk in baking. I love the Three Trees brand because their ingredients are simple and it's delicious. When making savory recipes, I tend to lean more toward half-and-half or sometimes even heavy cream because I think it really makes a difference in the finished dish and a little goes a long way. You just can't replicate that creaminess with almonds!

Eggs (pasture-raised): There's rarely a day that goes by that I don't eat eggs in some form. A veggie scramble in the morning, adding a hard-boiled egg to my protein bowl, topping a rice dish with a runny fried egg, and, of course, the million and one ways they work as recipe components, essential for breading or baking. All the recipes in the book call for large eggs and they'll stay fresh for weeks in the fridge. I pick them up from the farmers' market when I can, but Trader Joe's is also a great source, and of course your local supermarket.

Greens: A bag of baby spinach or mixed greens never goes to waste in my house. I love throwing spinach in my eggs, smoothies, pastas, and soups for an added nutrient boost. As for mixed greens, they're great for throwing together a last-minute side salad with dinner; an effortless way to make sure you're getting your daily veggies! You'll also find curly kale and baby arugula, plus an ingredient with an entire recipe to show it off: Little Gem Salad with Toasted Bread Crumbs and Creamy Calabrian Chile Dressing (page 140). Romaine is a hearty lettuce that can replace the Little Gem and it keeps well, too.

Herbs: Another amazing, healthy way to add flavor and color to your recipes is with fresh herbs. In the summer, I use a ton of basil, mint, parsley, and cilantro for their bright and fresh flavors. In the winter, I commonly use herbs that are a little more earthy, like rosemary, oregano, sage, and thyme. Although I am no stranger to using all the herbs listed year-round! If you have some outdoor space to grow them, all the better! And there are now these very cool indoor hydroponic "smart gardens," too.

Onions, garlic, and shallots: These are my lifeline, my holy trinity. I never make a trip to the grocery store without bringing at least one of them back home. They are the base of many recipes because they are versatile and packed with incredible flavor. I

am a big believer in using the fresh versions of these ingredients as opposed to garlic powder or onion powder (yes, I know, I have the powders in my spice list and those come in handy sometimes, too, like for marinades or the occasional sauce). One thing my mom instilled in me from a young age was to never use the finely chopped garlic that comes in a jar. I always thought she was silly, but now I totally understand. Fresh garlic has a bite and fragrance that are totally superior. I have to add green onions (scallions), too! Usually finely chopped or sliced thinly on an angle, these are in my Asian and Mexican dishes, stir-fries, rice bowls, tacos, or anytime I want a softer onion flavor with a slight crunch.

Freezer

Frozen fruit: I stock store-bought organic frozen fruit from both Trader Joe's and Whole Foods, especially when they are on sale, and when there's a bounty crop of blueberries in the summer I'll wash the berries, spread them out on parchment-lined trays or plates, and freeze and bag them so I have them year-round for smoothies or to use to replace the strawberries in the Strawberry Skillet Galette (page 239).

Frozen ginger: I also always keep frozen ginger cubes from Trader Joe's in my freezer. They're perfect to pop into smoothies or to make my Spicy Beef Rice Bowls (page 80) in a pinch.

Meat: If you haven't noticed by now, I love being able to make a meal from what I already have on hand because sometimes a trip to the grocery store sounds as daunting as running a marathon. Having frozen meat is often the key to saving yourself from an inconvenient grocery run, which means a yummy meal is just a short thaw away! I'll always have frozen steaks, pork chops, ground beef for Mom's Smashed

Burgers with Mac Sauce (page 143), ground turkey for my Turkey and Sweet Potato Skillet (page 119), and so much more. I'll even have ground lamb for White Bean Hummus with Spiced Ground Lamb (page 62). I practically have a shelf of boneless, skinless chicken breasts and thighs to use in more than a dozen recipes that I've included, and a package or two of chicken sausages for soups and bowls.

Shrimp: This is pretty much the only fish or shellfish that I don't buy fresh because the shrimp at the market is almost always previously frozen anyway. It's quick to thaw so you can easily cook up a skillet of Creamy Cajun Butter Shrimp (page 159) or a Crunchy Shrimp Roll Bowl (page 75).

Soups and broths: Making double batches, or even just one batch for me and freezing my soups in the freezer, has been life-changing for me! I use the Souper Cubes (see Kitchen Essentials, page 28) and they make thawing such a breeze because you can control the amount you're thawing rather than wrestling a ginormous block of soup!

Tequila: I firmly believe that a mixed drink should be icy cold! So you will find my tequila in the freezer for Grilled Pineapple Spicy Margaritas (page 228) and Tequila Negroni (page 215).

Veggies: Contrary to popular belief, frozen vegetables can be just as nutritious as fresh, plus they're more cost-effective. My faves are peas, corn, spinach, and cauliflower rice. I know, I know! I am a cauliflower rice hater most of the time, but I like it mixed in with regular rice or in soups and stir-fries because you can't even tell it's in there! I'll admit I actually prefer it to the usual orzo in the Greek-Style Lemon Chicken Soup (page 205). I keep the frozen corn for a number of recipes, but especially the Elote Nachos (page 38).

KITCHEN ESSENTIALS

As important as it is to have the right ingredients in your fridge, freezer, and pantry, having the right tools on hand—and handy—is essential, too. Subpar kitchen equipment only leads to confusing and sub-par meals, in my opinion. Plus, you'll spend a lot of extra time messing around in the kitchen when you could be enjoying time with your guests. There are also tools and appliances that are rarely used and just take up space (you will absolutely not find a cherry pitter or an ice cream maker in my precious storage space). Every home kitchen could benefit from a hard-core cooking gear inventory and re-org. Tools should be practical, easy to use, well made, and even inspirational—I can't wait to get into the kitchen and test out a new knife or a gorgeous skillet. But which styles are the dream blades you'll use every day and which are swipe lefts you can totally live without? I'm here to help you figure that out.

So, what do you need? Actually, not that much. Like my recipes, I like to keep tools simple, with some clever add-ons. Here's my list of the kitchen essentials you need (and none that you don't)!

Everyday Must-Haves

Pots and Pans

Dutch oven: My Le Creuset 5½-quart Dutch oven is one of the best investments I have made for my kitchen. I use it for everything from making soups and stews to braising meat or throwing together a one-pot meal. On the stovetop or in the oven, these pots deliver. There are a ton of different brands and options when it comes to Dutch ovens, and I know Le Creuset is expensive, but they're built to last a lifetime—and look pretty doing it. They're also a lot easier to clean than the cheaper ones I've used. But anything with some weight and a well-fitting lid will do you right for the most part!

10- and 12-inch cast-iron skillet: I couldn't live without my cast-iron skillets. They're essential when cooking with high heat. They're extremely durable and can withstand anything, plus they get beautifully nonstick once seasoned properly. Cast-iron is a must for getting a beautiful sear on a steak (try it out with my Perfect Cast-Iron Steaks with Crispy Cacio e Pepe Potatoes, page 156) or a crisp crust on your Pepperoni Cast-Iron Pan Pizza (page 165) or even for no-fail desserts like the Strawberry Skillet Galette (page 239). You can easily find one online for under forty dollars, or be like me and get the Our Place cast-iron skillet, which is enamel-coated so there's no seasoning and the upkeep is easier!

10-inch nonstick skillet with lid: But cast-iron isn't for everything, which is where a great nonstick pan comes in. This is probably the pan you'll reach for most to help with your everyday cooking, like frying eggs or reheating leftovers. It's lightweight and easy to clean, which is good because it never stays off the stove for long.

12-inch stainless steel skillet with lid: Nonstick pans shouldn't really be used when cooking with higher temperatures, so that's where a stainless steel pan comes in. Extremely versatile and great at holding heat, it's lightweight, and essential for beginning home cooks or experienced chefs alike. Most are ovenproof, too. I have a Material brand skillet and I love it.

3-quart saucepan with lid: This is the saucepan you'll use almost daily for making rice and/or sauces. I recommend one like mine, from Caraway.

5- or 8-quart saucepan with lid: When you need the capacity of a Dutch oven, but want to use a lighter pan that will bring things to a boil more quickly. They're the best for making pasta or quick soups. I have one from Our Place that I love!

Cutting and Prep

Grater: There's really no argument, freshly grating cheese will *always* be better than buying it already grated. But a good grater is no one-trick pony! A grater is also good for grating vegetables, like the cucumber that goes in my jalapeño tzatziki (see Sun-Dried Tomato and Feta Turkey Burgers with Jalapeño Tzatziki, page 115). Grating is also a fantastic sneaky hack for getting extra veggies like zucchini or carrots into pasta or stews. The classic box grater with different grating sizes on each of its sides has been around forever for a reason, but the handheld rotary grater is a nice item, too, especially for putting Parmesan on your pasta.

Knives: You see all those giant knife blocks, jam-packed with a bunch of blades, but I really only use three knives: a chef's knife for chopping and slicing almost everything, a paring knife for more precise cutting and peeling, like with small fruits and vegetables, and a serrated bread knife for bread (obvs) but also for tomatoes and even shaving chocolate. If there's a different kind of knife you love, go for it. But these three styles should be able to handle basically all of your cutting needs. Remember to keep them sharp. Nothing more frustrating (or potentially dangerous) than a dull kitchen knife. Material brand sells a great, small knife sharpener.

Kitchen shears: A sturdy pair of sharp kitchen shears can go a long way. I love using mine for destemming kale, cutting herbs, or spatchcocking a chicken (more details can be found with my recipe for Mediterranean Roasted Chicken with Homemade (or Not) Flatbread (page 163). Also, let's face it, there are a lot of packages to cut open these days and it's nice always knowing where to find a good pair of shears.

Measuring cups and spoons: I own some stacking measuring cups and spoons from Williams-Sonoma, but I definitely use my glass Pyrex measuring cups the most. They're a kitchen classic—super easy to use and clean. I use the 1-cup, 5-cup, or 8-cup Pyrex (which is very handy for soups). As far as measuring spoons, I have a supercute gold metal set that I found at some random little market, so remember you can find something to add character to your kitchen in all sorts of places! The square measuring spoons are also handy because even the tablespoon fits inside a supermarket spice jar. I prefer metal to plastic, since plastic can warp in the dishwasher.

Wooden cutting board: For prepping fruits and vegetables, or slicing bread or any other ready-to-eat foods, a sturdy wooden cutting board cannot be beat. Mine's pretty enough that it can even do double duty as a serving board! Great for laying out a charcuterie board, cheese and crackers, one of those IG-popular butter boards . . . anything you can think of. The bigger the better in this case.

Plastic cutting board: Anytime you're cutting meat, make sure you're using a plastic cutting board! I use the Material brand boards because they are made from recycled plastic and have a lifetime guarantee (the influencer in me is showing). I have two: a larger size for meat and a mini for quick jobs like slicing an apple or chopping some garlic. Just scrub with hot soapy water or pop in the dishwasher between uses.

Nesting mixing bowls: A set of mixing bowls will come in handy all day long, especially when prepping for a meal. I always cook with a scrap bowl nearby, which saves me a ton of time going back and forth from the counter to the trash (or better yet, the compost bin). My stainless steel nesting mixing bowls with lids from Umite Chef on Amazon are in constant use! Mixing batters, dressings, marinades—they also double as great food-storage containers.

Peeler: From peeling potatoes to cutting a twist of orange to drop into my Tequila Negroni (page 215), an old-fashioned peeler is an obvious kitchen staple. The simpler the better, in my opinion.

Sieves, colanders, and spinners: I use a regular stainless steel colander for washing salad, fruits, and vegetables, draining pasta, etc. You should also have a fine-mesh sieve for rinsing rice and straining stock, things like that. A salad spinner is also a necessity for my fellow salad lovers!

Appliances

Blender: I'm an immersion blender girl (see entry below) for most large jobs like soups, but day to day I tend to only use my single-serving blender from Beast Health (I also love a Nutribullet). As my poor Vitamix collects dust, my powerful little blender is a daily essential for making a morning smoothie or a quick vinaigrette.

Mixers: As someone who doesn't bake too often, I still think having either a stand mixer or an electric hand mixer is a must. It's a necessity for most baking recipes and the reason for choosing one over the other really just depends on budget and available counter space. A stand mixer can make your life a lot easier and do it in style, but a hand mixer will still get the job done.

Immersion blender: As I mentioned above, this is an absolute must for me, especially considering the amount of soups I make. Not only is this handy (literally!) tool perfect for blending up a soup right in the pot, you can use it to make sauces and creamy dressings, like the dressing on my Little Gem Salad with Toasted Bread Crumbs and Creamy Calabrian Chile Dressing (page 140).

8-cup food processor: I would absolutely love to tell you that a clunky food processor is not a necessary kitchen appliance, but I have to admit it is. I would never tell you to buy something you'll use once or twice, and I can promise you that if you cook your way through this book you will find a love and appreciation for the ultra-versatile food processor. You can use it to make sauces, like my homemade Basil Pesto (page 73) or to quickly mince vegetables. I bought a sixty-dollar Hamilton Beach food processor about three years ago and it still works like a charm!

Cooking Utensils

Metal tongs: I use these a lot because they're so versatile. From tossing salads to serving pasta to easy flipping, a set of metal tongs is a must.

Metal whisk: Every kitchen needs a good whisk, whether it's for baking or smoothing out sauces and gravy. There are many varieties, so choose the one that suits your need (and hand!). I also love my mini whisk from Material. It's so cute and maneuverable for smaller jobs, great for making super-creamy, lump-free sauces and dressings.

Offset metal spatula: You want these to be light but sturdy, because after the flipping and turning, it's also what you need to scrape stuck-on food bits from your cast-iron pan. I have one with slots that allows grease to drain through and another solid metal, perfect for flattening that ball of ground beef into the crusty brilliance of one of my Mom's Smashed Burgers with Mac Sauce (page 143).

Silicone spatula: Most commonly used for stirring my morning scramble, but also great for scraping, mixing, and always comes in handy when baking.

Great for getting every last bit out of a pan or mixing bowl.

Soup ladle: No explanation needed. A Soup Queen needs a soup ladle! Fun tip: You can use the ladle bowl like a measuring cup, too, as long as you know how much it holds. I use a 1-cup ladle.

Stainless steel large slotted spoon: Although I don't use this daily, I do think it's necessary to have. I use it mostly when boiling things like eggs or when making homemade broths. A large unslotted spoon also comes in handy when you don't want all the liquid to dribble through.

Wooden spatula/turner: Not a day goes by without me using my wooden turner. It's in my hand all day long stirring, sautéing, flipping . . . you name it. Plus, it won't scratch your nonstick pan or melt like a plastic one.

Baking

8-inch square baking pan: Brownies, bars, even mini casseroles are the perfect size when baked in one of these classic square baking pans.

9-inch round cake pan: Yes, for cakes, but I also frequently use mine for dips, like my Stuffed Mushroom Dip (page 49). I serve it in the pan, right out of the oven!

13 x 9-inch rectangular baking dish: From casseroles to roast chicken, a large baking dish will always come in handy, especially during the holiday season!

13 x 18-inch sheet pan: It's no secret that I love a sheet pan meal! The Texas Sheet Cake with Olive

Oil Chocolate Frosting (page 248) and Elote Nachos (page 38) are some of my favorite recipes, and they wouldn't be possible without my trusty, easy-to-clean sheet pan! Mine is from Caraway and it's also non-stick, which is a game changer! Half-size sheet pans are also great for warming up pizza or a muffin.

9 x 5-inch loaf pan: I should call this my banana bread pan because that's all I ever really use it for, but necessary nonetheless, especially for bread (obvs) or my mom's Spinach and Cheddar–Stuffed Meatloaf with Extra Sauce (page 184).

Parchment paper: Super handy to have for lining sheet pans and easy cleanup, a must for Mediterranean Fish in Parchment with Perfect Stovetop Rice (page 84), and great for Pavlova (page 241).

Silicone stuff: There are a million newer items made out of colorful, flexible silicone. Almost every baking pan has a silicone version, and baking on a flat silicone baking mat means zero cleanup for cookies, meringues, or candied nuts. You can even cook bacon on one. And I love the way the new silicone basting brushes never leave those stray hairs in your food.

Food Storage

Glass storage containers: I recently switched over to all-glass storage containers and it has been a game changer. You can bake or microwave in them, easily heat up leftovers, and they don't stain like plastic ones. Don't forget to order some small ones to store leftover sauces and dressings!

Souper Cubes: These silicone cube trays are such a storage and time-saving innovation! I absolutely love them for freezing soups, broths, and even smoothies. Just pop out your leftovers and heat them up! I get

them on Amazon and really can't recommend them enough.

Stasher silicone reusable storage bags: These BPA-free reusable bags from Stasher are essential for storing things like leftover meats and cheeses, fruit, sliced veggies, a sandwich you're taking to go . . . the list goes on! Plus, you can pop them in the dishwasher to clean!

Fun (but Necessary) Tools

Barware: For me, a cocktail shaker, jigger for measuring, and muddler to crush fruit for your drink are really must-have items if you want to make a fabulous cocktail.

Citrus press: Fresh citrus is a big part of my recipes and having a handheld citrus press makes getting the most out of your lemons and limes a breeze. It's also your best friend when throwing a cocktail party!

Garlic press: I don't always use this, but when a recipe calls for a lot of finely chopped garlic, this tool is a lifesaver. It's a little annoying to clean, but nothing expresses the essence of garlic better.

Instant-read thermometer: If you're uneasy about cooking meat (and even if you're not), an instant-read meat thermometer will change your life! It takes the guesswork out of cooking the perfect steak, roasts, fish . . . whatever . . . giving you confidence to get that expensive cut off the heat at just the right time. Most varieties are easily programmable for all varieties of protein and tastes. Thermapen is probably the gold standard, and there are even thermometers, like the Yummly, that you can program on your phone.

Meat masher: I've linked to this several times on my IG because I really love it! It breaks up ground meat with ease and doubles as a potato masher. Mine is Farberware and I got it on Amazon.

Microplane: Citrus zest adds a pop of freshness to sauces, salads, and marinades, and a Microplane rasp-style grater is the way to extract it. Great for getting garlic or ginger really small, I also use mine to finely grate Parmesan cheese so it comes out extra fluffy and melts on contact. Yum!

Pizza cutter: I debated if it was necessary to include this, but honestly I couldn't live without my pizza cutter. It comes in handy for a lot more than slicing pizza: I find it really helpful for cutting quesadillas, brownies, and for evenly cutting pita bread for my Seared Ahi Tuna with Homemade Pita Chips (page 53).

Olive oil spout: To ensure that olive oil doesn't just dump out all at once, a spout on top of your bottle of olive oil will give you more control over how much you're adding. So much more convenient than messing with the cap every time you want some olive oil (which, if you're making my recipes, should be a lot!).

Ratchet pepper mill: A friend gave me a ratchet pepper grinder from Sur La Table for my birthday and it has to be one of my favorite gifts ever. Nothing beats freshly cracked black pepper, and this mill makes it so easy—no more cramps from all that wrist twisting! Whether you need a little or a lot, you can also adjust the size of the cracked pepper, which I love.

Salt box: I buy my kosher salt in bulk, so I keep a beautiful marble salt box out on my counter that I go to all day long. Since pretty much every single recipe

that I've ever made calls for kosher salt, it's great to have easy access.

Silicone extra-large ice cube tray: Having a giant rectangular ice cube is 100 percent the way to make a big impression when serving a cocktail. It's the easiest way to look like a pro and a necessity for my Tequila Negroni (page 215) or La Vaquera (page 224).

QUICK TIPS

Think of this as your handful of Quick Tips to Kitchen Success. I'm not a big fan of those "you must do this!" scare tactics or any one-size-fits-all super-strict rules, but some key habits and insider tips will actually make your cooking go much more smoothly and set you up for success before you dive in. Just crucial bits of info and good habits I've picked up over the years that I find really useful in the kitchen. I learned some of these the hard way, so I'm happy to pass them along and save you the headaches. There are a million other tricks, techniques, and hacks out there—five minutes on TikTok shows you that—and you'll pick up all sorts of new things as you go along. But I think mastering the tips below will make your cooking better, less stressful, more fun, and the end result will be so good. Seriously, so good!

Basic knife skills: Slice, chop, dice, mince . . . What's the difference? I use these terms a lot and I've broken it down to be extra clear.

Slice: A cut across the length or width of something, varying in thickness depending on the effect you're going for. Most often called for with ingredients such as onions, zucchini, or carrots, or when slicing cooked and rested steaks.

Chop: A cut with each piece being similar in size, usually less exacting than dice, which is more precise and uniform. "Roughly chopped" is generally about ¾ inch while "chopped" is about ½ inch, and "finely chopped" is ¼ inch or slightly smaller, which is how I chop my herbs and garlic.

Dice: These are more precisely measured and carefully cut, because their presentation in the dish is important, or because they must cook at a more precisely even rate. Think of little pieces of carrot in a fancy sauce. The sizes are "large dice" (¾ inch), "medium dice" (½ inch), and "small dice" (¼ inch).

Mince: This is a very fine dice, the smallest you can cut, usually what you'll most often do with garlic, between ⅛ and ¹⁄₁₆ inch.

Mise en place: *Mise en place* is French for "put in place." This means gathering up the equipment and ingredients you're about to use in a recipe, measured, cut, and prepped so they're ready. This will *absolutely* change the way you cook and help you keep a clean space as you go.

You accomplish this by first reading through a recipe and then setting up your station:

- Start with a clean cutting board and set it over a wet paper towel—this keeps it from slipping around as you use it, which can be dangerous.

- Lay out all the knives and utensils you need.

- Set a medium bowl for garbage next to your cutting board so you're not dragging potato peels across the kitchen to throw them away.

- Measure, prep, and organize all the ingredients needed for the recipe.

- Get out the proper pots and pans you need before you even turn on the stove.

- And try to clean as you go! Waiting for the cake to bake or the fish to roast? Do a few dishes and wipe the counters in the meantime.

This way, you're setting yourself up for success before you even turn on the stove. If you've lined up everything you'll need before you even pick up your knife, you won't be scrambling looking for a missing ingredient as your chicken breast sits burning on the stove. If you feel like you're stressed in the kitchen, chances are you're not doing this!

Prep, prep, prep!: It's my mantra, which really makes cooking easier and more fun for me. Whether I am hosting a dinner party or making dinner for two, I love prepping as much as I can. Things that can always be done ahead of time are dressings, sauces, and desserts. I also love chopping everything ahead of time to keep a clean space.

Let's dish: One other thing I find *really* helpful is, if I'm having more than four people over, or if it's a special night, I try to get my dish act together ahead of time, too. Even if I don't set the table early, I try to choose my serving platters so I'm not scrambling for large enough plates, checking for enough glasses . . . they don't have to match but you do have to have enough! I also try to run the dishwasher before or at least have it empty so there's not a sink of dishes when friends are over. That makes me a little nutty honestly! Once everything is prepped and your mise en place is set up, you will be dancing your way to a perfect meal in no time at all!

Season to taste: You can cook each recipe in this book using the precise measurements I've given you, but you might still find that a dish could use a little salt or pepper, a touch of heat, or even a squeeze of fresh lemon to add some zip. This is the playful part of cooking! Trust yourself to cook to your personal needs. "Season to taste" means season to *your* taste. There is no wrong. There are so many variables in cooking—like the type of salt you use or where you're getting your produce—that I could never tell you *exactly* how to make a recipe. Always give it a taste for yourself before serving and trust yourself to make it the best version you can.

Have fun!: Consider the crowd, the time of event, time of year, and where you are. Don't overextend yourself and take on too much. One amazing dish is more impressive than a bunch of so-so ones. Keep the guest list small if you've had a busy week and aren't feeling that social. Trust yourself and—really important—cut yourself some slack. This isn't competitive entertainment. It's you doing you.

Cooking is my everything. I enjoy it more than anything in the world and my main goal is to have as many people as possible feel the same joy in the kitchen that I do! After practicing, prepping, and reading through the basic skills I have laid out for you, there is no reason you won't be successful in the kitchen.

So relax, enjoy the process.
You got this.

APPS, ALWAYS

Apps. Starters. Bites. Small plates. Regardless of what you call them, they're the foundation of my personal food pyramid, and usually my favorite part of a meal. My weekends are all about these small, enticing bites, because they're so flexible and easy, and a super-fun way to entertain. Invite some friends over, whip up some apps along with a great cocktail (see Cheers to That, page 213), and there's really not much more you need. No girls' night is complete without Panfried Brie with Pistachios and Rosemary Hot Honey (page 37) and a round of Spicy Rosé Spritzes (page 219). These apps bring happiness no matter where you live or what the season. While I'm fortunate to live in Southern California and hang out in the sunshine

most of the time, you can still get a taste of summer year-round anywhere, anytime, with a platter of Elote Nachos (page 38) and some Grilled Pineapple Spicy Margaritas (page 228). Best of all, when you're not quite sure what you want for dinner, a few apps can add up to an excellent meal. My White Bean Hummus with Spiced Ground Lamb (page 62) is almost a meal already, but when you add Seared Ahi Tuna with Homemade Pita Chips (page 53), you get a playful and flavorful version of surf and turf. You can't go wrong with upping the apps! This versatile chapter will help you plan a snack, cocktail gathering, lunch, dinner—even an all-out party— because these little dishes are always the star of the show. Apps, always.

Panfried Brie with Pistachios and Rosemary Hot Honey

SERVES 4 TO 6 / TOTAL TIME: 25 MINUTES

⅓ cup roasted and salted pistachios, shelled

⅓ cup panko bread crumbs

½ teaspoon kosher salt

¼ teaspoon freshly ground black pepper

1 large egg, beaten

1 (10-ounce) wheel Brie (or Camembert or similar washed rind cheese)

3 tablespoons extra-virgin olive oil

¼ cup Rosemary Hot Honey (recipe follows)

Sliced baguette or crostini (page 50), for serving

Sweet honey, herbaceous rosemary, and hot chiles form a love triangle that's also the perfect foil against the rich, creamy Brie and texture of the panko and pistachio crunch. I've never met anyone who's said no thanks to this one! (Except for the ones with nut allergies, so I often make a second one without the pistachios.) I always make triple the amount of Rosemary Hot Honey to keep around so I can drizzle it on everything from pizza to avocado toast. So damn good! I also have been known to add a cup of pitted mixed olives to the pan after the Brie, tossing them until they are warm, and then surround the cheese with the olives. Sometimes too much is never enough!

In a mini food processor or spice grinder, pulse the pistachios in 5-second intervals, until chopped, 10 to 15 seconds, taking care not to overprocess the nuts into a fine powder. Transfer the nuts to a wide shallow bowl and stir in the panko, salt, and pepper and evenly combine.

Add the beaten egg to a wide shallow bowl and set next to the bowl of pistachio bread crumbs. Dip the cheese in the beaten egg, coating all sides, and then dip and gently press the cheese into the breading mixture.

Heat the olive oil in a small skillet set over medium heat. When the oil begins to sizzle, add the cheese and cook until golden brown on both sides and soft in the center, about 3 minutes per side. Make sure to cook the outer ring of the cheese. Reduce the heat if the bread crumbs are beginning to darken too quickly. Transfer the cheese to a serving plate.

Add the honey to a microwave-safe bowl and microwave for 10 to 20 seconds until warm.

Using a honey dipper or small spoon, drizzle the Brie with the honey and serve immediately with the sliced baguette.

Rosemary Hot Honey

MAKES ¾ CUP

¾ cup honey

1 tablespoon finely chopped fresh rosemary

1 tablespoon red chile flakes

In a small bowl, combine the honey, rosemary, and chile flakes. If not using right away, store refrigerated in a tightly sealed jar for up to 2 weeks.

Elote Nachos

SERVES 6 / TOTAL TIME: 20 MINUTES

- ½ cup whole-milk plain Greek yogurt or sour cream
- 3 tablespoons mayonnaise
- Grated zest and juice of 1 lime
- ½ red onion, diced
- ⅓ cup chopped fresh cilantro, plus more for garnish
- 1 green onion, chopped
- ½ jalapeño, finely chopped
- 10 ounces tortilla chips
- 12 ounces shredded Mexican blend cheese
- 2 tablespoons extra-virgin olive oil
- 16 ounces frozen corn, thawed, drained, and patted dry
- 1 teaspoon chili powder
- ½ teaspoon sweet paprika
- ½ teaspoon kosher salt
- ½ teaspoon freshly ground black pepper
- Crumbled cotija or feta cheese for topping

This recipe was one of the earliest ones created for the book during a trip to Joshua Tree with my girlfriends. It reigns supreme because you can pull it off at the last minute—even several margaritas deep in a tiny Airbnb kitchen! Elotes are Mexican street-grilled ears of corn slathered in mayo or crema and topped with chili, lime, and salty cotija cheese, which has just the right bite to blast through the sweetness and spice. Here frozen corn steps in to take the place of fresh ears of corn so you can easily make this any time of year. Pour a pitcher of Grilled Pineapple Spicy Margaritas (page 228), Blackberry Mexican Mules (page 231), La Vaquera (page 224), lemonade, or crack open an ice-cold Pacifico!

Preheat the oven to 350°F. Line a sheet pan with foil.

In a large bowl, combine the yogurt, mayonnaise, lime zest, lime juice, red onion, cilantro, green onion, and jalapeño and stir to combine evenly. Set aside.

Spread half of the chips on the lined sheet pan without overlapping. Top with half of the shredded Mexican blend cheese. Top the cheese with a second layer of the remaining chips and cheese. Bake until the cheese is melted, 10 to 13 minutes.

Heat the olive oil in a large skillet over medium heat. Add the corn and cook, stirring occasionally, until warmed through, about 2 minutes. Add the chili powder, paprika, salt, and pepper, stir to evenly combine, and cook until the spices are fragrant, about 30 seconds. Transfer the corn mixture to the bowl with the yogurt mixture and stir to evenly combine.

When the nachos come out of the oven, top them with the corn mixture and sprinkle the cotija over everything. Garnish with chopped cilantro.

Extra-Extra-Virgin Olive Dipping Oil

SERVES 4 / TOTAL TIME: 10 MINUTES

¼ cup extra-virgin olive oil

2 tablespoons balsamic vinegar

1½ tablespoons grated Parmesan cheese

1 garlic clove, finely chopped

½ teaspoon red chile flakes

Kosher salt and freshly ground black pepper

½ loaf baguette or rustic country bread, sliced, for serving

Piatti in La Jolla, San Diego, is one of my all-time favorite restaurants. Mainly because I'm obsessed with the signature Parmesan/balsamic dipping oil they serve with their homemade bread. I call my version of it Extra-Extra because I'm so "extra," but really, it's because I order so much extra bread to keep dipping that I barely make it to my entrée—we've all been there! This dipping oil is an arsenal app because it's ready in a flash with ingredients right out of your pantry. It's ideal to serve when hanging with friends and drinking a bottle of red, a great first course before any pasta, or alongside a salad. Make sure to choose a quality extra-virgin olive oil, as it's the main star. Serve this with ciabatta, a baguette, or any rustic bread. Sometimes I like to add a sprinkle of chopped fresh rosemary or parsley, and you can round out the platter with chunks of Parmesan, grapes, and berries or figs, too.

In a small bowl, stir together the olive oil, vinegar, Parmesan, garlic, and chile flakes. Season with a pinch of salt and a few twists of pepper. Transfer the dip to a serving bowl and place on a platter surrounded by the sliced bread.

Marinated Olives and Manchego

SERVES 4 / TOTAL TIME: 10 MINUTES

1 (10-ounce) jar pitted Castelvetrano olives, drained

3 ounces Manchego cheese, cut into small chunks

1 garlic clove, finely chopped

2 tablespoons extra-virgin olive oil

1 tablespoon red wine vinegar

½ teaspoon kosher salt

¼ teaspoon freshly ground black pepper

¼ teaspoon red chile flakes

Grated zest of 1 lemon

Whenever I'm hanging out with friends, or even just making dinner for myself, a cheese and olive combo is always on tap. This savory pairing will no doubt become a signature app that can be made up to three days in advance. And unlike many other relationships, this one gets better as time goes on. My olive of choice is the green Sicilian Castelvetrano, a large, buttery, fruity, and slightly crisp olive that is not overly briny. The olives are well matched with the Spanish Manchego, a semifirm sheep's milk cheese with a subtle, slightly sweet, nutty, and buttery flavor. If you can't find Manchego, a milder choice would be Monterey Jack or a mild cheddar, and a bolder route would be chunks of Parmigiano-Reggiano. Use the best-quality EVOO (extra-virgin olive oil) you have. Be sure to taste the olive oil first, and if it is very peppery, you may want to reduce the amount of pepper the recipe calls for. Orange zest, instead of lemon, is great, too. Stir up a Tequila Negroni (page 215) or, for a lighter sip, a Spicy Rosé Spritz (page 219) to serve alongside.

NOTE

You can store these refrigerated in a sealed container for up to 3 days.

In a small bowl, add all the ingredients and stir to evenly combine. Refrigerate for 1 hour before serving. Remove from the refrigerator 15 minutes before serving.

ChuChukah (Roasted Red Pepper Dip)

SERVES 6 / TOTAL TIME: 1 HOUR

ROASTED PEPPERS AND GARLIC

2 green bell peppers, halved and seeded

2 red bell peppers, halved and seeded

4 tablespoons extra-virgin olive oil

Kosher salt and freshly ground black pepper

1 head garlic

DIP

2 tablespoons extra-virgin olive oil

2 (28-ounce) cans whole peeled tomatoes, undrained

½ teaspoon ground coriander

½ teaspoon ground cumin

¼ teaspoon cayenne pepper

¼ teaspoon ground cinnamon

2 teaspoons kosher salt

½ teaspoon freshly ground black pepper, plus more to taste

French bread, sliced, or toasted pita chips, for serving

NOTE

You can use fresh tomatoes if you'd like! Just boil them for 30 seconds, peel the skin off, and core them. You'll need about 2 pounds.

This recipe comes from my Moroccan grandmother, Meme. While we grew up pronouncing this dish "choo-tochoo-kuh," it's actually called *taktouka*, not to be confused with *shakshuka* (which is similar but has simmered eggs). This addictive dip's flavor is unleashed by roasting the peppers and garlic and then simmering them with tomatoes, chiles, and aromatic Moroccan spices, such as cumin, coriander, and cinnamon. If it's summer, try this with plum tomatoes or even large beefsteak tomatoes, peeled (either after blanching for 30 seconds or grilling for 1 minute or so per side). Any way you make this, you can't go wrong. Our family always serves this cold with crispy pita chips or sliced French bread. Thanks, Meme!

Roast the peppers and garlic: Preheat the oven to 375°F. Line a sheet pan with foil.

Place the bell peppers on the sheet pan and drizzle 2 tablespoons of the olive oil over both sides of the peppers. Season each side lightly with salt and pepper.

Slice off the top one-quarter of the head of garlic to expose the cloves. Drizzle with the remaining 2 tablespoons of the olive oil, wrap in a square of foil, and place alongside the peppers. Roast until the peppers are soft and charred and the garlic is softened, 35 to 40 minutes. Cover the pan with foil and allow the peppers to cool slightly. Peel the peppers.

Make the dip: Heat a Dutch oven over medium heat. Add the olive oil, tomatoes and their juices, and bell peppers. Squeeze the garlic out of their skins into the pan. Add the coriander, cumin, cayenne, cinnamon, salt, and pepper. Bring the mixture to a simmer, then reduce the heat to low and cook until the tomato flavor tastes rich and roasted, 45 to 55 minutes.

This dip is best served cold, so refrigerate it for at least 1 hour before serving.

Taste and add salt and/or pepper as needed. Serve with toasted pita chips or sliced bread and enjoy!

Citrus Salmon Crudo

SERVES 4 / TOTAL TIME: 10 MINUTES

Juice of ½ orange

Juice of ½ lime

1 tablespoon reduced-sodium soy sauce

½ tablespoon extra-virgin olive oil

½ teaspoon toasted sesame oil

½ teaspoon sriracha

5 ounces sushi-grade skinless salmon fillet (or store-bought salmon sashimi)

½ orange, cut into thin wheels

½ avocado, thinly sliced

2 tablespoons thinly sliced shallot

1 jalapeño, sliced into thin circles

2 tablespoons fresh cilantro leaves

Flaky sea salt and freshly ground black pepper

With all that life throws at us, I'm always on the lookout for a hack for recipes that are both super simple and deliver a big wow factor. I've even hacked the hack here by sometimes buying salmon sashimi from the sushi counter at the grocery store in place of the salmon fillet. No one will ever guess, based on how striking the presentation is, that this elegant app took less than 10 minutes to make. They'll be even more taken by the interplay of tangy citrus, salty soy, and the spicy sriracha set against the silky salmon and avocado. The only downfall is that you'll be extra annoyed the next time you have to fork over twenty-five dollars for the same dish in a restaurant, knowing how easy it is to make at home! This can also serve as a main course for a fancy lunch or a date night dinner.

Make the dressing: In a small bowl, stir together the orange juice, lime juice, soy sauce, olive oil, sesame oil, and sriracha. Set aside.

With a very sharp knife held at an angle to the cutting board, slice the salmon as thinly as you can. Arrange the orange wheels on the bottom of a serving plate or individual plates. Arrange the salmon, avocado, shallot, jalapeño, and cilantro on top of the orange wheels. Top with the dressing and sprinkle with flaky sea salt and a few twists of pepper.

Stuffed Mushroom Dip

SERVES 4 / TOTAL TIME: 25 MINUTES

2 tablespoons butter

16 ounces baby bella (cremini) mushrooms, chopped

1 tablespoon finely chopped fresh thyme leaves

8 ounces cream cheese

¼ cup whole-milk plain Greek yogurt

2 tablespoons grated Parmesan cheese

½ teaspoon kosher salt

¼ teaspoon freshly ground black pepper

½ cup shredded mozzarella cheese

2 tablespoons finely chopped fresh parsley, for garnish

Ritz crackers, for serving

The beauty of this recipe is that you won't spend all that time tediously stuffing each mushroom cap with grated cheese and herbs for a gooey, yummy bite. Now it all comes together in the superfast form of a dip. This leaves more time to make a round of drinks and gossip with the girls, and will also help you win over anyone who thinks they don't like mushrooms—swear!

I prefer baby bellas (also sold as creminis), because they have a deeper flavor than the familiar white buttons, but go ahead and use the buttons, shiitakes, portobellos, or a mix of the three. Perfect for a holiday potluck or a cozy date night app.

Preheat the oven to 400°F.

In an ovenproof skillet (I use cast-iron), melt the butter over medium heat. Add the mushrooms and thyme and cook, stirring, until the mushrooms are soft, 5 to 7 minutes. Add the cream cheese, yogurt, Parmesan, salt, and pepper and stir to combine.

Top with the mozzarella cheese and transfer to the oven. Bake until the cheese is melted and bubbling, 12 to 14 minutes.

Garnish with the parsley and serve with the crackers.

NOTE

If you don't have an ovenproof skillet, you can make the dip in a regular skillet up to covering with mozzarella. Then carefully transfer the dip to a baking dish, top with the mozzarella, and bake.

Goat Cheese Crostini with Tomato Confit

SERVES 4 / MAKES 12 TO 15 CROSTINI / TOTAL TIME: 1 HOUR

1 demi baguette, cut diagonally into ½-inch pieces

2 tablespoons extra-virgin olive oil

½ teaspoon flaky sea salt

4 ounces goat cheese (about ½ cup), at room temperature

½ cup Tomato Confit, room temperature (recipe follows)

Finely chopped fresh thyme leaves, for garnish

When I needed a quick app to whip up for our annual Girls' Christmas Party, I grabbed a few no-fail ingredients at Trader Joe's: bread, tomatoes, and cheese. While I wasn't expecting to make something cookbook worthy with just a few things, the speed at which these crostini disappeared earned them a spot in my favorite chapter. Once you master crostini, slices of crusty bread brushed with olive oil and a little salt and toasted or grilled, the possibilities are endless. They can be topped with anything from chopped tomatoes to a favorite cheese, to olive tapenade, to prosciutto. This version offers a slightly tart goat cheese layer covered with a sweet, jammy tomato confit. Crostini are also great for dipping in soups and sauces, like to soak up that delicious broth in my Cioppino Made Easy (page 193).

Preheat the oven to 425°F.

Brush the baguette slices with the olive oil and sprinkle with the flaky salt. Bake until golden brown and crisp, about 8 minutes.

Spread about 2 teaspoons of goat cheese on each crostini and top with a generous teaspoon of Tomato Confit. Top with thyme leaves to garnish.

NOTE

You can make the Tomato Confit ahead of time. If you're not, begin by making the Tomato Confit and transfer half of the confit (½ cup) for this recipe to a bowl to cool slightly (refrigerate the rest). I prefer to serve this at room temperature, not piping hot.

Tomato Confit

MAKES ABOUT 1 CUP / TOTAL TIME:
50 MINUTES

Use the confit as a spread for sandwiches, a topping for pasta, added to
omelets, or alongside grilled chicken
and fish. Or straight out of the jar, late at
night, in your jammies, leaning against
the fridge door. It's a great way to use
up the end-of-summer tomatoes and
a great trick for boosting flavor when
you're stuck with "meh" winter cherry
tomatoes. The herbs are a no-stress
choice; thyme is a more subtle choice,
or you can try a few rosemary sprigs for
a bolder confit or a sprinkling of fennel
seeds and hot chile flakes for an even
bigger impact. Leftovers (if you have
any) are great with a soft scramble for
breakfast.

¼ cup extra-virgin olive oil

16 ounces cherry tomatoes (about
2 cups)

3 garlic cloves, smashed and peeled

½ teaspoon kosher salt

¼ teaspoon freshly ground black
pepper

A few sprigs fresh thyme

Heat the olive oil in a medium skillet
over medium heat. Add the tomatoes,
garlic, salt, pepper, and thyme and
cook, stirring every few minutes,
until the tomatoes start to soften,
about 5 minutes. Reduce the heat to
low and cook, stirring occasionally,
until the tomatoes are jammy, 30 to
40 minutes. Let cool and store in the
fridge in a tightly sealed container for
up to 2 weeks.

Seared Ahi Tuna
with Homemade Pita Chips

SERVES 4 / TOTAL TIME: 45 MINUTES

MARINATED AHI

1 (8-ounce) piece best-quality ahi tuna

2 tablespoons reduced-sodium soy sauce

2 teaspoons toasted sesame oil

1 tablespoon avocado oil (or any oil with a high smoke point)

PITA CHIPS

2 pita bread

1 tablespoon extra-virgin olive oil

½ teaspoon flaky sea salt

SALAD

2 cups baby arugula or mixed greens

½ recipe Peanut Ginger Dressing (page 99)

2 tablespoons mayonnaise (Kewpie, if you can find it)

Sriracha and wasabi paste, for serving

½ jalapeño, thinly sliced

½ lemon, cut into wedges

Sesame seeds, for garnish

Short getaways to Mexico with my family or girlfriends help me recharge, reconnect, and get inspired. When I'm at home and heading toward burnout, I try to recall the sound of the surf and the sunsets and make this seared tuna dish inspired by a dish I had in Punta Mita for that staycation feel, although it works for any occasion. This is more of a small-plate app than finger food, with an ahi-jalapeño pita bite set off by a refreshing salad and can't-get-enough-of Peanut Ginger Dressing (page 99). Shop for top-quality fish; the freshness of the tuna is worth the cost for this recipe. You can buy baked pita chips if you don't have time to make them yourself. Complete your relaxation with Grilled Pineapple Spicy Margaritas (page 228) or a Vodka Watermelon Spritz (page 221).

Preheat the oven to 375°F. Line a sheet pan with foil.

Marinate the ahi: Add the ahi to a large dish or plastic bag. Pour the soy sauce and sesame oil over the ahi and turn over a few times to combine. Marinate in the refrigerator for 20 minutes while you prep.

Bake the pita chips: Brush both sides of the whole pita with the olive oil and sprinkle with the flaky salt. Cut each pita into 8 wedges and arrange on the lined sheet pan. Bake until crispy on the outside and soft on the inside, 7 to 9 minutes.

Cook the ahi: Heat the avocado oil in a well-seasoned cast-iron or medium skillet over medium-high heat. When the oil is almost smoking hot, add the ahi and sear for 1 minute on each side. The middle should still be pink and very rare! Slice the ahi into thin slices, then cut in half to fit on each pita chip.

To assemble the salad: Toss the greens in the dressing and place in the middle of the serving plate. Spread the mayonnaise on the pita triangles and assemble the triangles in a circle around the salad. Dot the sriracha and wasabi paste around the plate.

Place a piece of ahi on each pita and top with a jalapeño slice. Squeeze lemon juice on top and sprinkle with sesame seeds. Serve immediately.

Moroccan-Spiced Carrots with Whipped Feta

SERVES 4 TO 6 / TOTAL TIME: 35 MINUTES

1 pound large carrots, peeled

1 teaspoon ground cumin

1 teaspoon kosher salt

½ teaspoon sweet paprika

½ teaspoon ground turmeric

¼ teaspoon chile flakes

¼ teaspoon ground ginger

⅛ teaspoon ground cinnamon

2 tablespoons extra-virgin olive oil

4 ounces feta cheese (about ¾ cup)

⅓ cup whole-milk Greek yogurt

1 tablespoon extra-virgin olive oil

1 garlic clove, roughly chopped

¼ teaspoon kosher salt

⅛ teaspoon freshly ground black pepper

Lime wedges for squeezing

Fresh parsley leaves, for garnish

I am a sucker for any type of sweet, succulent roasted carrot and when you pair it with some salty whipped feta . . . I'm done for. With this dish, I transformed my dream app into reality, and roasted carrots go from supporting cast members to the opening act, or in this case, the opening app. The carrots are tossed with ground ginger, cinnamon, earthy paprika, and turmeric to take them from bland to bold with exotic Middle Eastern flavors. The sweet roasted carrots on top of a swirl of whipped feta, yogurt, and garlic transform this into a small plate you'd find at a restaurant that's harder to get into than a Taylor Swift concert. The whipped feta can be made a day or so ahead and stored in a tightly sealed container in the refrigerator, and it's also pretty tempting as a solo act on a cracker! I love to serve it with my Extra-Extra-Virgin Olive Dipping Oil (page 40) with extra bread for dipping in the whipped feta.

Preheat the oven to 425°F. Line a sheet pan with parchment paper.

Make the Moroccan-spiced carrots: Halve the carrots lengthwise, and cut them crosswise into 1½- to 2-inch lengths. In a large bowl, combine the cumin, salt, paprika, turmeric, chile flakes, ground ginger, cinnamon, and olive oil. Add the carrots to the spice mixture and stir until evenly coated.

Arrange the carrots on the lined sheet pan in a single layer. Bake until they are slightly crisp and soft on the inside, 20 to 25 minutes.

Meanwhile, make the whipped feta: In a small food processor, combine the feta, yogurt, olive oil, garlic, salt, and pepper. Blend until fluffy, about 1 minute.

Spread the whipped feta evenly on the bottom of a large shallow bowl or serving platter. Arrange the carrots on top. Add a squeeze of lime juice and garnish with the parsley.

Bacon, Date, and Goat Cheese Dip

SERVES 6 / TOTAL TIME: 30 MINUTES

10 ounces goat cheese (about 1¼ cups)

½ cup whole-milk Greek yogurt

2 tablespoons honey, plus more for drizzling

2 tablespoons grated Parmesan cheese

½ teaspoon kosher salt

¼ teaspoon freshly ground pepper

6 slices uncured bacon

8 Medjool dates, pitted and chopped

2 tablespoons chopped fresh rosemary

Red chile flakes, optional

Baguette slices, for serving

I'm always trying to take a recipe that's been a hit on my blog or Instagram and play with it to deliver even more flavor and time-saving tips for the Broccolinis. Guys, I'm happy to say I nailed it with this one! The original Bacon-Wrapped Dates with Goat Cheese and Honey from my blog are damn good, and now this version gives you the same salty, sweet, crispy flavors without the finicky finger work. You can get a head start by whipping the goat cheese a day ahead, stashing it in a sealed container in the fridge, and lightly whisking it the next day before continuing with the rest of the recipe. I amped up the flavor by adding grated Parmesan and rosemary, too, and you can add some chile flakes for heat, if that's your thing. You really can't go wrong!

In a food processor, combine the goat cheese, yogurt, honey, Parmesan, salt, and a few twists of pepper. Blend until smooth and fluffy, about 1 minute. Transfer to a serving bowl.

Line a large plate with paper towels. Arrange the bacon in a large cold skillet. Set over medium heat and cook until the bacon is crispy, 8 to 10 minutes, flipping the slices midway. Transfer the bacon to the paper towels to drain. Carefully pour all but 1 to 2 tablespoons of the bacon fat out of the skillet. (Alternatively, you can also bake the bacon on a wire rack set in a sheet pan in a preheated 375°F oven until crispy, 15 to 20 minutes. Transfer 1 to 2 tablespoons of bacon fat from the sheet pan to a skillet to continue with the recipe.)

Add the dates and rosemary to the bacon fat in the skillet over medium heat and cook, stirring occasionally, until the dates are warm, about 2 minutes.

Sprinkle the dates and rosemary mixture over the whipped goat cheese. Crumble the bacon over the dates and drizzle with some honey and sprinkle with red chile flakes (if using). Serve with baguette slices for dipping.

Cheesy Garlic Bread with Warm Marinara

SERVES 4 / MAKES ABOUT 15 SLICES / TOTAL TIME: 20 MINUTES

- 1 stick (4 ounces) unsalted butter, at room temperature
- ¼ cup grated Parmesan cheese
- 4 garlic cloves, finely chopped
- 3 tablespoons finely chopped fresh parsley
- ¼ teaspoon kosher salt
- ¼ teaspoon freshly ground black pepper
- ¼ teaspoon red chile flakes, plus more for serving
- 1 baguette (about 15 inches), halved lengthwise
- ½ cup shredded mozzarella cheese
- 3 cups jarred marinara sauce (preferably Rao's)

This is the MVP, crowd-pleaser app for any situation, no-fail, no-fuss, ingredients always on hand, and never disappoints. It works for guests of any age, and for unexpected ones. It's just the thing for late at night, or with drinks, and of course alongside any pasta—especially Quick Rigatoni Bolognese (page 68) or Spicy Lasagna Soup (page 197). Don't skip the parsley; it's an underrated herb that adds a fresh peppery note to the garlic butter and richness of the mozzarella. You can make these a day ahead and keep them in the fridge; just be sure to take them out so they are room temperature before you bake them. I've been known to keep an oven-ready prepped loaf in the freezer "for company," and by that, I mean myself and a movie. Garlic bread can be dinner, too, if you need it to be!

Preheat the oven to 400°F.

In a small bowl, using a fork, combine the butter, Parmesan, garlic, parsley, salt, pepper, and chile flakes until smooth. Spread the garlic butter evenly on the cut side of each piece of the bread.

Set the buttered bread on a sheet pan and loosely cover the top of the bread with a sheet of foil. Bake for 10 minutes. Remove the foil and top with the mozzarella. Bake until the cheese is bubbling and slightly browned, about 6 minutes. If the cheese doesn't have those nice crispy browned bits, place the bread under the broiler for about 1 minute.

Meanwhile, in a small saucepan, heat the marinara sauce over medium heat. Transfer the marinara to a serving bowl.

Cut the bread into 1-inch-thick slices on the diagonal and place the slices on a platter along with the bowl of marinara. Pass extra chile flakes for sprinkling!

Chicken Dumplings
with Spicy Soy Dipping Sauce

SERVES 4-6 / MAKES 24 DUMPLINGS / TOTAL TIME: 45 MINUTES

DIPPING SAUCE

4 tablespoons reduced-sodium soy sauce

2 teaspoons rice vinegar

2 teaspoons toasted sesame oil

2 teaspoons honey

2 teaspoons sriracha or chili crisp

DUMPLING DOUGH

1 cup all-purpose flour, plus more for dusting

1 large egg white, lightly beaten

Pinch of kosher salt

6 tablespoons warm water

FILLING

½ pound ground chicken

4 garlic cloves, finely chopped

1½ tablespoons grated and peeled fresh ginger

2 green onions, chopped (about 4 tablespoons)

1½ tablespoons reduced-sodium soy sauce

3 teaspoons toasted sesame oil

1 teaspoon rice vinegar

½ teaspoon kosher salt

¼ teaspoon red chile flakes

Canola oil for panfrying (1 to 2 tablespoons per batch)

I love a classic dinner party, but every once in a while, you need to spice things up. Instead of the usual dinner, I host a dumpling night. It's a great way to keep everyone's hands busy and their phones down! Everyone gets involved (and messy), and it leads to some of my favorite memories. While you can buy prepared wonton wrappers, I hope you'll also give making them from scratch a try. Make a double batch, freeze half, and pop them in a steamer for a quick snack or last-minute dinner. Sake, beer, and jasmine tea are mandatory.

Make the dipping sauce: In a small bowl, combine the soy sauce, vinegar, sesame oil, honey, and sriracha and stir to evenly combine. Set aside.

Make the dough: Dust a large cutting board or work surface with flour. In a large bowl mix the flour, egg white, and salt. Slowly pour in the warm water, a little at a time, stirring to combine the dough. Once the dough is combined, place it on the floured surface to knead until smooth. Cover the dough with a kitchen towel and let it rest while you make the filling.

Make the filling: In a large bowl, combine the ground chicken, garlic, ginger, green onions, soy sauce, sesame oil, vinegar, salt, and chile flakes. Gently mix to evenly combine.

Fill and cook the dumplings: Set out a small bowl of warm water. On a lightly floured workspace, knead the dough once or twice so it is smooth, and cut it into 6 pieces. With a rolling pin, gently roll out each piece of dough into a long thin rope and cut the rope into 4 pieces. Roll each piece into a ball and then, using a rolling pin, roll the ball to form a 3-inch round wrapper, about 1⁄16 -inch thick.

Add about 1 tablespoon filling slightly off-center on a wrapper. Dip your fingers in water, then dampen the rim of the wrapper and fold the wrapper over to form a half-moon shape. Fold or pleat the edges to seal. Continue until all of the dumplings are filled and wrapped.

You can boil or steam the dumplings, but I prefer to panfry and steam them. Heat a drizzle of canola oil in a large skillet over medium heat. Add enough dumplings to fit nicely in the pan without overcrowding. Add about 3 tablespoons of water to the pan, cover, and cook until the bottom is crispy and the middle is cooked through, 6 to 8 minutes. Repeat with remaining dumplings and serve with the dipping sauce.

White Bean Hummus with Spiced Ground Lamb

SERVES 4 / TOTAL TIME: 30 MINUTES

WHITE BEAN HUMMUS

¼ cup tahini

3 tablespoons extra-virgin olive oil

Juice of 1 lemon

1 garlic clove, peeled

1 (15-ounce) can Great Northern beans, drained and rinsed

¼ cup ice-cold water, plus more as needed

1 teaspoon kosher salt

½ teaspoon ground cumin

¼ teaspoon freshly ground black pepper

CRISPY LAMB

2 tablespoons extra-virgin olive oil, plus more if needed

½ yellow onion, diced

2 garlic cloves, finely chopped

½ pound ground lamb or beef

1 teaspoon kosher salt

½ teaspoon freshly ground black pepper

½ teaspoon ground cumin

½ teaspoon sweet paprika

½ teaspoon dried oregano

¼ teaspoon ground cinnamon

¼ teaspoon ground coriander

⅛ teaspoon cayenne pepper

FOR SERVING

Extra-virgin olive oil, for drizzling

1 tablespoon finely chopped fresh parsley

1 teaspoon finely chopped fresh mint

Toasted pita bread or chips or sliced crusty bread

This is always the standout of a mezze spread when I make a Middle Eastern dinner. The milder and creamier white beans replace the more typical chickpea hummus and are topped with spiced crispy lamb and a shower of chopped fresh mint and parsley. Ground lamb has a richer flavor than beef and is just as versatile. Try it as a sub in your taco or pasta recipes, and buy an extra pound to stash in your freezer. Serve this sans lamb with Mediterranean Roasted Chicken with Homemade (or Not) Flatbread (page 163) or with store-bought pita chips, and make extra hummus for the vegetarians in your group. This one always has my friends licking the bowl clean! And yes, that is more than acceptable in my house.

Make the white bean hummus: In a food processor or blender, combine the tahini, olive oil, lemon juice, and garlic and process until blended, about 1 minute. Add the white beans, ice water, salt, cumin, and pepper and blend until smooth and creamy, about 1 minute. Add additional water if needed. Transfer to a large shallow serving bowl and set aside while you prepare the lamb.

Make the crispy lamb: Heat the olive oil in a large skillet over medium heat. Add the onion and cook, stirring occasionally, until the onion is translucent, about 5 minutes. Add the garlic and cook, stirring frequently, for 30 seconds to 1 minute, taking care not to burn the garlic. Increase the heat to medium-high and add the lamb. Season with the salt, pepper, cumin, paprika, oregano, cinnamon, coriander, and cayenne and stir. Let

the lamb sit and cook, undisturbed, to brown and crisp for 2 to 3 minutes. When crisp, using a large spatula, flip the lamb and continue to cook and crisp the other side for 2 to 3 minutes. Break up the lamb into smaller pieces and continue to stir and cook the lamb until even crispier, 1 to 2 minutes longer, adding more oil if needed. The

lamb should be fully cooked and not pink. Season with additional salt and pepper if needed.

Place the lamb mixture on top of the hummus and drizzle with olive oil. Garnish with the parsley and mint. Serve with toasted pita bread or chips or bread slices.

DINNER
IN 30

There's a lot of talk about having a full, rich life and balance. For me that means not always ordering in, but not standing in front of the fridge picking or eating a yogurt standing at the counter, either. That's where Dinner in 30 came from. I think one of my three manifest wishes would be the power to create dinners with the snap of my fingers. While I haven't managed that yet, I've gotten pretty close to getting my wish just the same. These are the recipes that come together faster than picking up from your local take-out joint. There's no shortcut on the flavor they deliver, and whatever mood you're in I promise there's a dish here for you. Coconut Fish Tacos with Mango Salsa (page 79) for when a vacation feels too far away after a long day at work. Or get that daylong simmered taste of a classic Sunday sauce quicker than most podcasts take to get started with a Quick Rigatoni Bolognese (page 68). A last-minute meeting throw off your dinner plans? Luscious, chewy Sheet Pan Gnocchi with Burst Cherry Tomatoes and Pesto (page 72) will give you that pasta-fix you crave in less time than it takes to heat up leftovers. These are dishes you'll want to cook even when you have more time, especially my Date Night Chicken in Creamy Mushroom Sauce (page 71) for a seductive stay-in. But the best part is that while these recipes are all fast and easy to make, you can have more time to do you, which for me usually means sneaking in an afternoon nap or more time to dig into my Colleen Hoover book.

Quick Rigatoni Bolognese

SERVES 6 TO 8 / TOTAL TIME: 30 MINUTES

2 tablespoons kosher salt

16 ounces rigatoni, or pasta of choice

¼ cup extra-virgin olive oil

1 medium yellow onion, finely diced

1 carrot, peeled and finely diced

2 garlic cloves, finely chopped

1½ teaspoons kosher salt

¼ teaspoon freshly ground black pepper

½ pound ground beef, 85% lean (or your fat preference, no judgments!)

½ pound ground pork

1 (6-ounce) can tomato paste

1 tablespoon balsamic vinegar

1 (28-ounce) can crushed San Marzano tomatoes, undrained

⅓ cup half-and-half

¼ teaspoon red chile flakes

Grated Parmesan cheese, for serving

Finely chopped fresh parsley or basil, optional

It doesn't have to take all day to make an impressive Bolognese, and this recipe proves it. While this rich, complex sauce may taste like it's been simmering on the stove for hours, it'll be on the table before you finish your glass of Cab Sauv (my wine of choice with this meal). It's so good, in fact, you'll want to make a double batch and freeze half for those nights after work when even half an hour seems like too much prep time. The combination of pork and beef gives the sauce an extra depth, but feel free to use all beef or all pork if you prefer. The balsamic is the secret replacement for time here—the aged vinegar adds a deeper level of flavor that stands in for the hours and hours of simmering you get to skip! Before the hour's up you'll find me cozy on the couch with a massive bowl, big glass of red wine, the fireplace lit, and a rom-com on. Probably with some Salty, Crunchy Fudge (page 245) for a sweet treat. If that's not an ideal night, then we have different ideas of a good time.

Bring a large pot of water and the salt to a boil. Add the pasta to the boiling water and cook to al dente according to the package directions.

Meanwhile, heat the olive oil in a Dutch oven or large pot over medium-high heat. Add the onion and carrot and cook, stirring occasionally, until softened, about 2 minutes. Add the garlic, salt, and pepper, and cook until the garlic is softened and fragrant, 30 seconds to 1 minute.

Add the beef and pork and use a wooden spoon or spatula to break up and flatten the meat so it is evenly covering the bottom of the pan. Let it cook, undisturbed, until browned, about 2 minutes. Reduce the heat to medium, stir the meat to break it up, and add the tomato paste and vinegar. Stir to evenly coat the meat and

cook, stirring occasionally, until the tomato paste darkens and the sugars caramelize, 1 to 2 minutes.

Add the crushed tomatoes and juices, half-and-half, and chile flakes, stir to combine, and continue to cook, stirring occasionally until the pasta is ready.

When the pasta is done, scoop out ½ cup of the pasta water and reserve. Drain the pasta and stir it into the sauce. Vigorously stir in the reserved pasta water. Taste for seasoning and adjust as needed.

Transfer to individual serving dishes or a large serving bowl and top with Parmesan. If desired, garnish with fresh parsley or basil.

Panfried Zucchini Pasta

SERVES 4 / TOTAL TIME: 25 MINUTES

2 tablespoons extra-virgin olive oil

1 cup panko bread crumbs

1 teaspoon Italian seasoning

¼ teaspoon kosher salt

¼ teaspoon freshly ground black pepper

3 tablespoons grated Parmesan cheese

PASTA

1 tablespoon kosher salt

8 ounces spaghetti

2 cups jarred marinara sauce (preferably Rao's)

ZUCCHINI

Extra-virgin olive oil, for frying

3 medium zucchini, sliced into ¼-inch-thick rounds

½ teaspoon kosher salt

½ teaspoon freshly ground black pepper

Generous pinch of red chile flakes

Have you ever been to an Italian restaurant that serves fried zucchini instead of bread when you sit down? It's the most unexpected treat you can ever hope to be lucky enough to experience. When my stars align and I'm given the opportunity to pregame my meal with some crispy zukes, I always save some to top my pasta for that ideal combo of light crunch that every pasta dish needs, almost like a surprise veggie bread crumb. And now you can have that same restaurant blissed-out experience. This easy fried zucchini uses a simple panfried panko coating to amp up the crunch, without having to individually bread each piece (nobody has time for that!). If you cut the zukes too thickly, the natural water content will make them soggy, so slice them carefully into ¼-inch-thick rounds (use a mandoline to create evenly thin pieces for craveable crispy zucchini). Just try to not eat them all straight out of the pan . . . Now that's heaven.

Make the crispy bread crumbs: Heat a large skillet over medium-low heat. Add the olive oil, panko, Italian seasoning, salt, and pepper. Cook, stirring, until the panko is golden, about 3 minutes. Remove from the heat and transfer to a bowl. Stir in the Parmesan and set aside. Wipe the pan clean so you can use this for the zucchini.

Cook the pasta: Bring a large pot of salted water to a boil. Add the pasta and cook to al dente according to package directions. Drain, do not rinse, and return to the pot. Add the marinara sauce and toss to coat. Cover to keep warm.

Meanwhile, fry the zucchini: Add some olive oil to the same large skillet you used for the panko. For my large pan I use about 3 tablespoons per batch. Set the pan over medium-high heat. Working in batches to avoid crowding the pan, add the zucchini rounds in a single layer. Dividing evenly (depending on how many batches you are cooking; it could take up to 3 batches), sprinkle with the salt, pepper, and chile flakes. Let the zucchini cook and sit undisturbed for 45 seconds to 1 minute before turning to crisp. Flip the zucchini and allow to cook and sit undisturbed for 1 minute before turning again. Continue to cook, turning the zucchini occasionally, until they are tender inside and crispy on the outside, 5 to 6 minutes. Set aside on a large plate or sheet pan. Continue to cook the remaining zucchini, adding additional olive oil as needed.

Divide the pasta among 4 bowls and top with the zucchini and crispy bread crumbs.

Date Night Chicken in Creamy Mushroom Sauce

SERVES 4 / TOTAL TIME: 30 MINUTES

2 boneless, skinless chicken breasts (about 1½ pounds)

1½ teaspoons kosher salt

¼ teaspoon freshly ground black pepper

2 tablespoons extra-virgin olive oil

5 tablespoons unsalted butter

3 large shallots, thinly sliced

4 garlic cloves, finely chopped

12 ounces baby bella (cremini) mushrooms, thinly sliced

3 tablespoons fresh thyme leaves

½ tablespoon balsamic vinegar

2 tablespoons all-purpose flour

1¼ cups chicken broth

¾ cup half-and-half

¼ cup grated Parmesan cheese

Juice of 1 lemon

¼ cup finely chopped fresh parsley, for garnish

1 lemon, quartered, for squeezing

Crusty rustic bread, toasted, or steamed Perfect Stovetop Rice (page 84), for serving

This is the best chicken dish I've ever made. You will want to lick the skillet clean, the sauce is so damn good! I upped the recipe so there's enough to dunk plenty of bread in or to serve over rice. While this dish is a big wow, the ingredients are far from fancy. The baby bella mushrooms (aka creminis) have a lighter flavor than portobellos and a richer flavor than white buttons (don't stress—white shrooms play nicely). Congrats! You've just mastered a restaurant pan sauce, which you can flex on pork chops, steak, or fish fillets. Go ahead, lick the skillet—just promise me you'll let the pan cool down first!

With a chicken breast flat on the cutting board, make a horizontal cut into the fat side of the breast and slice the breast hozrizontally in half to make 2 cutlets. Repeat with the second breast. Cover with a layer of plastic wrap and use a meat mallet or a small heavy skillet to lightly pound the cutlet to an even ½-inch thickness. Season both sides of the chicken with ½ teaspoon of the salt and ¼ teaspoon black pepper.

Heat the olive oil in a 10-inch skillet with about 2-inch sides or a large Dutch oven over medium heat. Add the chicken, in batches if necessary, and cook until cooked through, 2 to 3 minutes per side. Remove the chicken to a plate and set aside.

Reduce the heat to medium-low and add the butter, shallots, and remaining 1 teaspoon salt and cook, stirring, until lightly golden, 1 to 2 minutes. Add the garlic and cook, stirring frequently, until golden and lightly fragrant, 30 seconds to 1 minute, taking care not to burn the garlic. Increase the heat to medium, stir in the mushrooms and thyme, and cook until the mushrooms are soft, 6 to 8 minutes. Stir in the vinegar and cook for 1 minute, stirring occasionally.

Reduce the heat to medium and sprinkle in the flour. With a wooden spoon, cook, stirring frequently for 30 seconds to 1 minute to lightly toast the flour. Add the chicken broth, half-and-half, and Parmesan and stir to combine. Bring the sauce to a simmer and cook until the sauce has thickened, 1 to 2 minutes. Stir in the lemon juice, return the chicken and any juices to the pan, and gently rewarm the chicken for 30 seconds to 1 minute.

Transfer to a platter, top with a few grinds of pepper, and garnish with the parsley. Serve with lemon quarters and a big slice of crusty bread or on top of Perfect Stovetop Rice (page 84).

Sheet Pan Gnocchi with Burst Cherry Tomatoes and Pesto

SERVES 2 / TOTAL TIME: 30 MINUTES

1 (16-ounce) package uncooked shelf-stable potato gnocchi

1 pint cherry tomatoes (about 3 cups)

2 tablespoons extra-virgin olive oil

1 teaspoon dried oregano

¾ teaspoon red chile flakes

1 teaspoon kosher salt

½ teaspoon freshly ground black pepper

2 cloves garlic, finely chopped

½ cup Basil Pesto (recipe follows)

1 cup arugula

2 tablespoons grated Parmesan cheese

Finely chopped fresh basil or parsley, for garnish

1 lemon, cut into wedges, for squeezing

While I know that being a food blogger implies that I am always in the kitchen, whipping up some intricate meal, when it comes to making weeknight dinner for myself, I can be pretty lazy. So when making a quick dinner a sheet pan is my BFF. I can mix everything right on the pan, including the gnocchi, and it all cooks quickly and evenly, and you can serve it all straight from the pan! Roasting the tomatoes brings out their sweetness, and the fresh nutty pesto, which can be made while the gnocchi bake, pulls it all together. That said, please know that there is NO shame in using store-bought pesto so you have more time to take a shower or call your mom. The walnuts lend a more rustic texture and deeper flavor than traditional pine nuts, plus they're usually more affordable, but by all means, use pine nuts if that's your jam. Use the ½ cup of leftover pesto as a spread on sandwiches, grilled fish or chicken, or when you make this again, two days later lol! You can up the protein and have extra for guests or leftovers by adding some sliced sausage to the pan.

Preheat the oven to 425°F.

Spread the gnocchi and cherry tomatoes in a 13 x 18-inch sheet pan. Drizzle with the olive oil and sprinkle with the oregano, chile flakes, salt, and pepper. Toss to coat evenly. Roast for 10 minutes.

Add the garlic, toss to combine, and roast until the tomatoes are blistered and soft and the gnocchi are lightly browned and crispy on the outside, 12 to 15 minutes. Set the pan aside to cool slightly.

Meanwhile, make the Basil Pesto as directed (see recipe opposite).

Toss the gnocchi and tomatoes with about 3 tablespoons of the pesto right on the sheet pan.

Plate on individual serving plates or a large platter. Top with the arugula, a few more tablespoons of pesto, Parmesan, fresh basil or parsley, and a squeeze of lemon (don't skip this part!).

Basil Pesto

MAKES 1 CUP

2 cups packed fresh basil leaves

¼ cup grated Parmesan cheese

3 tablespoons walnuts or pine nuts

1 garlic clove, roughly chopped

½ teaspoon kosher salt

Freshly ground black pepper

½ cup extra-virgin olive oil, plus more if needed

In a food processor, combine the basil, Parmesan, walnuts, garlic, salt, a few twists of pepper, and 2 tablespoons of the olive oil and pulse 3 to 4 times. While the machine is running, slowly drizzle in the remaining oil for about 30 seconds. The pesto should have a little texture and not be too oily. If it appears dry, transfer to a small bowl, and stir in more oil, 1 tablespoon at a time, until the mixture is easily spreadable and moist.

Crunchy Shrimp Roll Bowl

SERVES 2 / TOTAL TIME: 30 MINUTES

SPICY MAYO

1 cup short-grain sushi rice

¼ cup mayonnaise

2 teaspoons sriracha

2 teaspoons toasted sesame oil

¼ teaspoon kosher salt

CRISPY SHRIMP

½ pound small shrimp (about 20 shrimp), peeled and deveined

⅓ cup coconut flour or all-purpose flour

1 teaspoon kosher salt

¼ teaspoon freshly ground black pepper

2 large eggs

1½ to 2 cups panko bread crumbs

Avocado oil

BOWLS

¼ cup grated carrots (about 1 carrot, peeled)

½ cucumber, cut into thin 2-inch matchsticks (about ½ cup)

½ avocado, thinly sliced

Sesame seeds or furikake seasoning, for garnish

2 tablespoons finely chopped green onions, for garnish

2 tablespoons spicy mayo

Reduced-sodium soy sauce, for serving

Sriracha, for serving

Crunchy shrimp rolls, with their satisfying crunch and spicy-sweet flavor, fuel a craving that's grown into a deep and abiding sushi obsession. This recipe takes the best parts of the roll—sweet, crunchy shrimp, veggies, and spicy mayo—and puts them into an easy-to-make, fun-to eat, satisfying bowl. Make a double batch of the spicy mayo; you'll love it spread on sandwiches or as a dip for veggies. I've worked out the strategic timing here, so if you begin making the rice first, you can finish the rest of the meal as it cooks. Look for furikake at your local Asian market or Trader Joe's, or online. This Japanese seasoning blend of sesame, nori, sugar, and salt makes the dish soar. Prepare to be obsessed!

Make the rice: Rinse the rice with cold water in a fine-mesh sieve and add to a small saucepan along with 1 cup of cold water. Let sit for 15 minutes. Bring the rice to a boil over medium heat, cover, reduce the heat to low, and simmer for 10 minutes. Remove the rice from the heat and let sit, covered, for an additional 10 to 15 minutes. Fluff with a fork.

Make the spicy mayo: In a small bowl, whisk together the mayonnaise, sriracha, sesame oil, and salt. Set aside.

Meanwhile, make the crispy shrimp: Set out a large plate or sheet pan with paper towels to hold the shrimp after panfrying.

In a shallow bowl, whisk together the coconut flour, salt, and pepper to evenly combine. Beat the eggs in a second shallow bowl. Place the panko in a third shallow bowl.

Dredge the shrimp in the seasoned coconut flour and lightly pat the flour on both sides. Tap off any excess. Dip the shrimp one by one in the egg to cover, then allow any extra egg to drip back into the bowl. Place the shrimp in the panko and turn to coat and transfer to a large plate.

Heat enough avocado oil to generously coat the bottom of a large skillet over medium heat. Working in batches to avoid crowding the pan, add 5 to 7 shrimp to the hot oil and cook until golden brown and cooked through, 2 to 3 minutes on each side. Transfer to the paper towels. Continue until all of the shrimp are cooked, wiping out the pan as needed and adding more oil.

To assemble the bowls, divide the rice, carrots, cucumber, and avocado evenly between 2 bowls. Arrange the shrimp on top of one side of the rice. Top with sesame seeds or furikake, green onions, and spicy mayo. Pass soy sauce and sriracha at the table.

Sheet Pan Blackened Salmon Bites with Potatoes, Broccoli, and Creamy Cilantro Sauce

SERVES 4 / TOTAL TIME: 30 MINUTES

CREAMY CILANTRO LIME SAUCE

⅓ cup whole-milk Greek yogurt

2 tablespoons extra-virgin olive oil

Grated zest and juice of 1 lime

1 cup fresh cilantro leaves

1 garlic clove, peeled but whole

1 teaspoon kosher salt

BLACKENED SALMON

2 teaspoons light brown sugar or coconut sugar

2 teaspoons sweet paprika

1 teaspoon garlic powder

1 teaspoon kosher salt

½ teaspoon ground cumin

½ teaspoon dried oregano

½ teaspoon freshly ground black pepper

¼ teaspoon red chile flakes

1½ pounds salmon, skinned and cut into 1- to 1½-inch cubes

2 tablespoons extra-virgin olive oil

VEGETABLES

4 red potatoes (about 8 ounces), cut into ½-inch chunks (about 2½ cups)

4 tablespoons extra-virgin olive oil

Kosher salt

Freshly ground black pepper

4 cups broccoli florets (about ½ pound)

1 lemon, sliced, for serving

Yes, another sheet pan classic, sue me. But you all know they're my go-to for a reason! This is one of the most flavor-bomb recipes in this chapter, plus it's one of the fastest to clean up, two very critical things in my world of cooking! This is the solution for an intimate dinner party dish that gives you plenty of time to hang with your guests and still serve something amazing. It has also become a weeknight staple in my house for when I'm feeling the urge for something hearty but healthy. Make sure to give the potatoes a bit of a head start in the oven since it takes longer for the skins to crisp up, then add the broccoli and fish for a quick roast. The creamy cilantro sauce is another staple for me, really amsping up grilled meats, veg, fish, grain bowls, and tacos—pretty much everything it touches! The blackened seasoning mix also works well on pork tenderloin or boneless, skinless chicken thighs. And while you have the oven on you may as well whip up a batch of Flourless Espresso Brownies (page 235) for an easy and impressive dessert.

NOTE

Make sure you cut your potatoes up into small chunks. This will ensure they cook in the allotted amount of time. If you prefer a bigger piece of potato, cook them for another 5 to 10 minutes before adding the salmon and broccoli.

Preheat the oven to 400°F.

Make the creamy cilantro lime sauce: Add the yogurt, olive oil, lime zest and juice, cilantro, garlic, and salt to a small food processor or blender and blend until smooth, about 1 minute. Refrigerate until ready to serve.

Prepare the blackened salmon: In a large bowl, stir together the brown sugar, paprika, garlic powder, salt, cumin, oregano, pepper, and chile flakes. In a large bowl, gently toss the salmon cubes with the oil and dip the salmon pieces into the spice mix to

evenly coat all sides. Place on a plate and refrigerate until ready to cook.

Place the potatoes on a large sheet pan and drizzle with 2 tablespoons of the olive oil. Season with ½ teaspoon of the salt and a few twists of pepper and toss to combine. Bake for 6 minutes.

Remove the pan from the oven. Carefully set the broccoli next to the potatoes on the pan, drizzle the remaining 2 tablespoons of the oil over broccoli, and sprinkle with ¼ teaspoon of the salt and a few twists of pepper. Use tongs to toss to combine.

Place the salmon next to the broccoli.

Return the pan to the oven and bake until the salmon is opaque through to the center, 8 to 10 minutes. If you prefer your fish on the rarer side, with the flesh slightly translucent at the center, go for the shorter time.

Transfer the salmon, potatoes, and broccoli to individual plates and drizzle with some of the cilantro lime sauce. Garnish with lemon slices. Pass the remaining sauce at the table.

Coconut Fish Tacos with Mango Salsa

SERVES 2 / TOTAL TIME: 30 MINUTES

MANGO SALSA

1 mango, chopped

1 cucumber, peeled and chopped

½ jalapeño, finely chopped (seeded for less heat)

½ red onion, finely chopped

½ cup finely chopped fresh cilantro

Juice of 1 lime

½ teaspoon kosher salt

½ teaspoon freshly ground black pepper

CRISPY COCONUT FISH

1 cup coconut flour

2 large eggs

1 cup panko bread crumbs

¾ cup unsweetened shredded coconut

1 teaspoon kosher salt

½ teaspoon freshly ground black pepper

4 tilapia fillets (4 ounces each) or another mild, firm white fish, such as mahi mahi

3 tablespoons avocado oil, plus more as needed

ASSEMBLY

4 large flour tortillas (9- or 10-inch) (I use Siete Almond Flour Tortillas) or corn tortillas

Hot sauce, optional

Lime wedges for squeezing

NOTE

Want to switch it up? Ditch the tortillas and serve the fish and mango salsa over brown rice with some avocado.

Two of my favorite things on this earth are fish tacos and coconut shrimp. And they are made even better when they're found in my favorite place on earth, Cabo! A few summers ago down there, when I was a couple of margaritas deep, I felt like I'd died and gone to heaven when I spied coconut fish tacos on the menu of a hole-in-the-wall restaurant on the beach. It. Was. Perfection. Upon reentry to the real world, I decided to replicate the recipe so we could all enjoy those post-beach vibes, no matter where we'd spent our day. Coconut flour lends a sweet nutty flavor here while adding a lighter texture to the batter than the usual all-purpose flour, but if you don't have it, just sub in cornstarch instead. I also prefer unsweetened shredded coconut because the sweetened variety is usually too sweet. And, obviously, I'd suggest you pair these with one of my refreshing cocktail recipes like my Grilled Pineapple Spicy Margaritas (page 228), which will definitely have you feeling those tipsy beach vibes.

Make the mango salsa: In a bowl, stir together the mango, cucumber, jalapeño, onion, cilantro, lime juice, salt, and pepper. Taste and adjust the seasoning if needed. This can be done the day before if kept in a sealed container in the refrigerator.

Make the crispy coconut fish: Set up a breading station with 3 shallow bowls. Add the coconut flour to a shallow bowl. Beat the eggs in the second bowl. In the third bowl, stir and evenly combine the panko, coconut, salt, and pepper. Gently press each side of the fish fillet in the coconut flour and lightly pat the flour on both sides. Tap off any excess. Dip the fillets one by one in the egg to cover, then allow any extra egg to drip back into the bowl. Place the fillets in the panko/coconut mixture and turn to coat then transfer to a large plate.

Heat the avocado oil in a medium skillet over medium heat. Work in batches if the fish fillets won't all fit in the pan at once. Add the fish to the hot pan and cook until golden brown and the fish is opaque when pierced with a knife in the center, 3 to 4 minutes on each side. If working in batches, wipe the pan, adding more oil if necessary. Set the fish on a serving platter or individual plates.

Wrap the tortillas in a damp paper towel and either microwave for 15 to 30 seconds or warm in the pan on the stovetop. Serve the fish, mango salsa, hot sauce (if using), and lime wedges with the warmed tortillas.

Spicy Beef Rice Bowls

SERVES 4 / TOTAL TIME: 20 MINUTES

SAUCE

⅓ cup reduced-sodium soy sauce

2 tablespoons honey

1 tablespoon rice vinegar

1 tablespoon toasted sesame oil

2 tablespoons Thai sweet chili sauce or sriracha

SPICY BEEF

1 tablespoon avocado oil

2 green onions, thinly sliced

1 tablespoon grated and peeled fresh ginger (about a 1½-inch piece)

3 garlic cloves, finely chopped

1 pound ground beef, preferably 85% lean

1 teaspoon kosher salt

½ teaspoon chili powder or ⅛ teaspoon cayenne pepper

BOWLS

2 cups Perfect Stovetop Rice (page 84)

1 cucumber, thinly sliced

1 green onion, thinly sliced, for garnish

Sesame seeds, for garnish

Chili crunch oil or sriracha (optional), for serving

When I know I have a busy week coming up, I'll often make a double batch of rice on Sunday for some stress-free twenty-minute lunch or dinner options throughout the week. I can always count on these bowls to recharge me on any given day. If you've stocked up from the Grocery Run list (page 11), this meal comes together in a snap. With some avocado oil, green onions and ginger in the fridge, and ground beef (chicken or turkey works, too!) in the freezer, you'll be able to make this on the regular without having to leave the house. You can endlessly tweak the vibe here by adding things like store-bought kimchi or topping it with apple salsa (from Pork Chops with Apple Salsa, page 90). A crispy fried egg with a runny, creamy yolk will take this bowl over the top (not to mention making it even more photogenic!), while adding an extra hint of protein to help you rule your day.

Make the sauce: In a small bowl, whisk together the soy sauce, honey, vinegar, sesame oil, and chili sauce. Set aside.

Make the spicy beef: Heat the avocado oil in a large skillet over medium heat. Add the green onions, ginger, and garlic and cook, stirring frequently, until fragrant, 1 to 2 minutes. Increase the heat to medium-high, add the beef, salt, and chili powder, and use a wooden spoon to break up and spread out the meat. Let the meat cook undisturbed for 1 to 2 minutes to brown. Using a spatula, flip the beef over and cook for another 30 seconds to brown. Add the sauce and simmer, stirring occasionally, until most of the liquid is absorbed, about 5 minutes. Remove from the heat.

Assemble the bowls: Scoop ½ cup rice into 4 individual bowls. Dividing evenly, spoon the beef onto one half of the bowl. Add the cucumber to the other side. Garnish with the green onion and sesame seeds. Top with chili crunch or sriracha like I do if desired!

Mediterranean Fish in Parchment with Perfect Stovetop Rice

SERVES 4 / TOTAL TIME: 20 MINUTES

4 skin-on firm white skinless fish fillets (6 ounces each), such as halibut, cod, or tilapia

Kosher salt

Freshly ground black pepper

2 garlic cloves, finely chopped

2 shallots, thinly sliced

1½ cups cherry tomatoes, halved

½ cup pitted green olives (I prefer Castelvetrano), chopped

⅓ cup finely chopped fresh parsley

Grated zest and juice of 1 lemon, plus 4 lemon slices

⅓ cup extra-virgin olive oil

3 cups Perfect Stovetop Rice (page 84), for serving

Lemon wedges for squeezing

Here's one of those unicorn kinds of meals: You put some gorgeous fresh ingredients in a little packet and a few minutes later, voilà, you have dinner! While this is one of my cherished wow-the-guests kinds of dinner party meals, it's also an easy weeknight dinner. It's healthy, too, so win, win, and win! Fish in parchment is one of those things that sounds intimidating (props to the chef!) but is actually quite simple. Honestly, it's close to foolproof. The most important thing is getting the freshest fish you can find. The buttery Castelvetrano olives (my absolute favorites) really work with this dish, as they aren't super salty and briny like other varieties, but feel free to use what you like or have on hand. The wow part comes when the simple folds of parchment balloon up in the oven like a cloud, just waiting to be opened up and enjoyed with a Spicy Rosé Spritz (page 219) . . . or two.

Preheat the oven to 400°F.

Lay out 4 sheets of parchment paper each about 13 inches long. With a long side facing you, fold the paper in half like a book to make a center crease and open them back up. Place a fish fillet skin-side down on the center of the right-hand side of each packet. Lightly season the fish with salt and pepper. Dividing evenly, top the fish with the garlic, shallots, tomatoes, olives, and parsley. Sprinkle with the lemon zest and drizzle with the lemon juice. Top with a lemon slice

and drizzle with the olive oil. Fold the left-hand side of parchment over the fish to meet the edge on the right side. Begin tightly folding/pleating in around the edges to create a small packet roughly in the shape of a half circle.

Transfer the packets to a sheet pan and bake until the fish is cooked through, 10 to 12 minutes. To serve, transfer packets to the 4 plates so guests can carefully open them, and serve rice to add to the packets to soak up the juices, along with more lemon wedges.

Perfect Stovetop Rice

MAKES 3 CUPS

1 cup jasmine rice

Pinch of kosher salt

½ yellow onion, sliced through the root

2 tablespoons unsalted butter

Bring 2 cups of water to a boil in a medium lidded pot over high heat.

Meanwhile, rinse the rice in a fine-mesh sieve until the water runs clear.

Add the rice to the boiling water and when it returns to a boil, add the salt and onion half. Cover, reduce the heat to low, and simmer until the liquid is absorbed, about 20 minutes.

Remove the onion. Add the butter and cover until melted, about 30 seconds. Fluff with a fork and serve!

Cherry Tomato and Goat Cheese Orzo

SERVES 4 / TOTAL TIME: 30 MINUTES

3 tablespoons extra-virgin olive oil

1 large shallot, thinly sliced

2 garlic cloves, finely chopped

1 pound cherry tomatoes

1½ teaspoons kosher salt, plus more to taste

½ teaspoon red chile flakes

12 ounces asparagus, cut into ½-inch pieces (about 2 cups)

1 tablespoon balsamic vinegar

1 (15½-ounce) can Great Northern white beans, drained and rinsed

1 cup dried orzo

½ cup goat cheese (4 ounces), plus ¼ cup (2 ounces), for garnish

½ cup fresh basil leaves, thinly sliced into ribbons, plus more for garnish

Juice of ½ lemon

Freshly ground black pepper

This easy vegetarian one-pot meal will no doubt be your new go-to when you're in need of a cozy escape but can't quite get to the Mediterranean! If you've followed my Grocery Run shopping strategy (page 11), you likely already have most of the ingredients in your pantry and fridge. Orzo, the often overlooked dried pasta, is the unsung hero here. It's just the right size to simmer along with the vegetables and warm beans, providing a tenderer and silkier base than a typical pasta or rice, almost like a risotto. The goat cheese also amps up the creaminess. This recipe is really flexible—if you can't find basil, add a teaspoon of fresh rosemary or oregano, or a tablespoon of dried Italian seasoning. Perfect as a meatless, filling meal with a big glass of your favorite red or transforms a simple fish fillet, like my Mediterranean Fish in Parchment (page 83), into a restaurant main course. Wherever it takes you, I'm sure it will work its way into your regular rotation.

Heat the olive oil in a large Dutch oven or pot over medium heat. Add the shallot and garlic and cook, stirring occasionally, until fragrant, about 2 minutes. Add the tomatoes, salt, and chile flakes and cook, stirring occasionally, until the tomatoes begin to burst, 3 to 4 minutes. Add the asparagus and cook, stirring occasionally, until the tomatoes are completely soft, about 3 minutes longer. Stir in the vinegar and bring to a simmer. Stir in 2 cups of water, the white beans, and orzo and bring to a boil. Reduce the heat to low, cover, and cook until most of the water has been absorbed, 15 to 20 minutes.

Stir in the goat cheese, basil, and lemon juice and season to taste with black pepper and additional salt, if needed.

Transfer to a serving bowl and garnish with the remaining goat cheese and some fresh basil.

One-Pot Chicken Pasta

SERVES 4 / TOTAL TIME: 30 MINUTES

2 boneless, skinless chicken breasts (about 1½ pounds) cut into bite-size pieces

1 tablespoon Italian seasoning

1 teaspoon garlic powder

1 teaspoon kosher salt

½ teaspoon freshly ground black pepper

3 tablespoons extra-virgin olive oil

1 small yellow onion, diced

2 garlic cloves, finely chopped

½ cup oil-packed thinly sliced sun-dried tomatoes

3 cups chicken broth

½ cup half-and-half

8 ounces penne pasta

2 cups (3 ounces) baby spinach

½ cup grated Parmesan cheese, plus more for serving

3 tablespoons finely chopped fresh parsley, for garnish

I've seen my fair share of creamy chicken pasta dishes on IG, and I'm always intrigued . . . until I read the recipe: tons of butter, cream, and other ingredients that I usually avoid during the week, as they tend to weigh me down. This lightened-up alternative is what I came up with to satisfy that craving without having to take a nap afterward. It's just the right balance of lean protein, veggies, carbs, and healthy fats without dairy overload. This dish gets its zip from something you'll always find a jar of in my fridge: sun-dried tomatoes (they're also a key player in Sun-Dried Tomato and Feta Turkey Burgers with Jalapeño Tzatziki on page 115). Cooking all of the elements of the pasta in the same pot—one of my favorite tricks—is a double win: The pasta absorbs the flavors of the sauce and one less pot to clean!

Season the chicken with Italian seasoning, garlic powder, salt, and pepper.

Heat 2 tablespoons of the olive oil in a Dutch oven or pot over medium-high heat. Add the seasoned chicken and cook, turning the chicken occasionally, until no longer pink in the center, about 4 minutes. Set the chicken on a plate.

Add the remaining 1 tablespoon of olive oil to the pan and reduce the heat to medium. Add the onion and garlic and cook, stirring occasionally, until the onion is translucent, 5 to 7 minutes.

Add the sun-dried tomatoes, chicken broth, and half-and-half. Bring the mixture to a boil. Reduce the heat to low, add the pasta, bring to a simmer, cover, and cook until the pasta is al dente, stirring occasionally, 13 to 15 minutes. If the liquid absorbs before your pasta is cooked, add more broth.

Stir in the chicken, spinach, and Parmesan. Serve garnished with parsley and more Parmesan.

Bean and Cheese Enchiladas

SERVES 4 / TOTAL TIME: 30 MINUTES

ENCHILADA SAUCE

3 tablespoons all-purpose flour or gluten-free flour

1 tablespoon chili powder

1 teaspoon ground cumin

½ teaspoon garlic powder

½ teaspoon dried oregano

½ teaspoon kosher salt

½ teaspoon freshly ground black pepper

⅛ teaspoon ground cinnamon

2 tablespoons avocado oil

2 tablespoons tomato paste

2½ cups vegetable broth

½ teaspoon apple cider vinegar

ENCHILADA FILLING

1 tablespoon avocado oil

½ yellow onion, diced

2 cups chopped spinach

1 (16-ounce) can refried black beans

1 tablespoon Taco Seasoning (page 97) or store-bought

ASSEMBLY

8 (10-inch) tortillas (I like Siete Almond Flour Tortillas), corn or flour

2 cups shredded Mexican blend cheese

⅓ cup finely chopped green onions, plus more for garnish

Sour cream, for serving

I tend to remix my favorite foods to suit my tastes, and these Bean and Cheese Enchiladas are the perfect example. Beans and cheese are my ride-or-die combo and it's one of my favorite dishes to serve for a hungry crowd or for a meatless Monday meal prep. Refried black beans are my favorite, but I can totally get behind refried pintos, too. The homemade enchilada sauce here is practically effortless and uses a small dash of cinnamon for that secret ingredient that adds the "I can't quite place it, but I also can't stop eating it!" effect. Enchiladas are one of the best ways to use up leftovers, so feel free to roll up any cooked chicken or roasted vegetables hanging out in the fridge. I'm sure by now you've noticed I'm partial to almond flour tortillas, but flour or corn ones work just as well. Humblebrag here, but I do think my recipe for Taco Seasoning (page 97) beats the packaged stuff, but if you want to go with store-bought, I totally get it!

Preheat the oven to 375°F.

Make the enchilada sauce: In a small bowl, stir together the flour, chili powder, cumin, garlic powder, oregano, salt, pepper, and cinnamon.

Heat the avocado oil in a saucepan over medium heat. Add the flour mixture and whisk until smooth. Add the tomato paste and continue whisking. Slowly whisk in the vegetable broth and cook, whisking occasionally, until the mixture is thick, about 5 minutes. The mixture will thicken as it cools. Remove from the heat, stir in the vinegar, and set aside.

Make the enchilada filling: Heat the avocado oil in a large skillet over medium heat. Add the onion and cook, stirring occasionally, until softened, about 5 minutes. Add the spinach and cook, stirring, until wilted, about 1 minute. Stir in the refried beans and taco seasoning.

Roll 'em up: Coat the bottom of a 13 x 9-inch baking pan with the enchilada sauce and transfer the remaining sauce to a wide shallow baking dish or bowl. Spread the tortillas out on the work surface. Dividing evenly, spoon the filling on one end of each tortilla. Roll the tortillas up, dip each filled tortilla carefully into the enchilada sauce, and place them seam-side down in the baking dish. Generously pour the remaining enchilada sauce over the top to coat all of the tortillas. Top with the cheese and green onions.

Bake until the cheese starts to bubble, 15 to 20 minutes. Let cool slightly and serve with green onions and sour cream on the side!

Pork Chops with Apple Salsa

SERVES 4 / TOTAL TIME: 25 MINUTES

APPLE SALSA

4 boneless pork loin chops (4 to 5 ounces each), about ½ inch thick

1 Gala apple, diced

1½ cups cherry tomatoes, quartered

1 small shallot, diced

3 tablespoons roughly chopped fresh cilantro

Juice of ½ lime, or more to taste

1 tablespoon extra-virgin olive oil

½ teaspoon ground coriander

½ teaspoon kosher salt

¼ teaspoon freshly ground black pepper

PORK CHOPS

1 tablespoon all-purpose flour

2 teaspoons chili powder

2 teaspoons garlic powder

2 teaspoons sweet paprika

1 teaspoon ground cumin

1 teaspoon kosher salt

1 teaspoon freshly ground black pepper

3 tablespoons avocado oil

Pork chops and applesauce is a dinner mantra for a good reason—the combination is undeniable. I grew up eating this favorite duo, thanks to my mother, whose version is the very definition of comfort food. Wanting to modernize it a bit, I swap out the jarred applesauce for sweet-tart apple salsa and quickly sear the pork, rather than cook with more traditional methods that leave it tough, dry, and overcooked. I rely on my instant-read thermometer for perfect doneness: 145°F is what you're aiming for here. It's easy to make it gluten-free if you omit the flour (or swap in a gluten-free all-purpose flour). Also, no shame in using a store-bought Cajun spice blend or another favorite. This is a meal in itself, but you can always serve it with rice, potatoes, or any carb you'd like. The apple salsa is also a bright sidekick to the Spicy Beef Rice Bowls (page 80).

Remove the pork chops from the refrigerator, pat dry with paper towels, and set aside.

Make the apple salsa: In a medium bowl, combine the apple, tomatoes, shallot, cilantro, lime juice, olive oil, coriander, salt, and pepper. Stir to combine. Taste and add more salt or lime if needed, depending on the sweetness of your apples.

Pork chop o'clock: In a large shallow bowl, stir together the flour, chili powder, garlic powder, paprika, cumin, salt, and pepper. Press both sides of the pork chops into the seasoned flour and set aside.

Heat the oil in a large cast-iron skillet over medium heat until almost smoking. Add the pork chops, being careful not to let them touch each other, leaving about an inch between each chop to ensure they get a crispy crust. Cook in batches, if necessary. Cook the pork chops until crisp and an instant-read thermometer inserted horizontally through the center of the chop reads 145°F, about 3 minutes per side. Remove the pork chops from the pan and let rest for 2 to 3 minutes before serving. Serve with a generous scoop of the apple salsa.

FEEL GOOD FOOD

I'm constantly redefining what it means to be "healthy." For me, it's managing my anxiety with morning meditation, moving my body in a way that makes me feel strong and powerful every day, and of course fueling my body with feel-good food. That doesn't mean denial or dieting, because I don't believe any of that contributes to a healthy lifestyle. I believe in delicious food that nourishes your body, mind, and soul. My philosophy is to eat well and eat what you want. There is a definite link between mood and food, and for maintaining my active lifestyle, these are some of the recipes I rely on. We're talking grain bowls, salads, skewers, satays, even tacos! Nutrient-packed, easy, and full of great flavor, these are the dishes I eat when I'm already feeling good or want some help getting there. Chicken Satay and Kale Salad (page 98) or my classic girls' night go-to Pistachio Pesto Salmon (page 112) are great for a midweek boost or the perfect dishes to crush after a hike in Malibu—but you'll crave them whenever. The best part of these sustaining and satisfying recipes is that they don't require a special trip to the natural food store to find some obscure ingredient. This chapter is packed with everything from full-on vegetarian dishes to sizzling fish to burgers, all of which will help you keep your body and mind in the best mood.

Hawaiian-Style Chicken Bowls with Pineapple and Macadamia Nut Slaw

SERVES 4 / TOTAL TIME: 45 MINUTES

MARINATED CHICKEN

¼ cup pineapple juice (see Note)

2 tablespoons reduced-sodium soy sauce

¼ cup ketchup

3 garlic cloves, finely chopped

2 tablespoons coconut or brown sugar

2 tablespoons sriracha

1 tablespoon apple cider vinegar

¼ teaspoon freshly ground black pepper

1½ pounds boneless, skinless chicken breasts or thighs, cut into bite-size pieces

PINEAPPLE AND MACADAMIA NUT SLAW

3 tablespoons toasted sesame oil

2 tablespoons pineapple juice (see Note)

2 tablespoons reduced-sodium soy sauce

1 tablespoon rice vinegar

Grated zest and juice of ½ lime

Freshly ground black pepper

8 ounces store-bought coleslaw mix or shaved cabbage

1 cup diced pineapple

¼ cup coarsely chopped fresh cilantro

2 green onions, thinly sliced

½ jalapeño, diced (seeded if you prefer less heat)

½ cup roasted and salted macadamia nuts, chopped

Kosher salt, to taste

BOWLS

2 tablespoons avocado oil

3 cups Perfect Stovetop Rice (page 84), for serving

Sesame seeds for garnish, optional

I talk a lot about mood and food with my Broccolinis, and this easy bowl comes up whenever someone's looking for a boost. If ever there was such a thing as an edible Hawaiian sunset, this is it! The heft comes from chicken marinated in a spicy sweet sauce and stir-fried, while the crunchy refreshing slaw of pineapple and macadamia nuts is guaranteed to lift my gray days. The slaw is an ideal companion for grilled fish, shrimp, scallops, piles of more veggies, like asparagus and spinach, and your favorite rice bowl, including the Spicy Beef Rice Bowls (page 80). You can swap the macadamias for cashews if you need to, but try and splurge if you can.

Marinate the chicken: In a large zip-seal plastic bag or sealable container, mix together the pineapple juice, soy sauce, ketchup, garlic, sugar, sriracha, vinegar, and pepper. Add the chicken and marinate in the refrigerator for at least 30 minutes or up to overnight.

Make the slaw: In a large bowl, whisk together the sesame oil, pineapple juice, soy sauce, vinegar, lime zest, lime juice, and a few twists of pepper. Mix in the coleslaw mix, pineapple, cilantro, green onions, and jalapeño. Set the macadamia nuts aside (they don't go in until serving time). Refrigerate the slaw while you prepare the chicken and rice.

Heat the avocado oil in a large skillet over medium heat. Remove the chicken from the marinade and reserve the marinade. Add the chicken pieces to the pan, and cook until a slight crust is formed, about 2 minutes on each side. Add the reserved marinade to the skillet and bring to a simmer. Reduce the heat and cook until the sauce has thickened and the chicken is cooked through, about 2 minutes.

Assemble the bowls: Stir the reserved macadamia nuts into the slaw mix, and add salt to taste. Divide the rice among 4 bowls. Set the chicken over the rice with a side of slaw. Sprinkle with sesame seeds, if desired.

NOTE If using fresh pineapple juice, add ¼ teaspoon brown or coconut sugar to the mixture.

Crispy Mushroom Tacos

SERVES 4 / TOTAL TIME: 30 MINUTES

CILANTRO-LIME SLAW

½ cup whole-milk Greek yogurt

2 tablespoons fresh lime juice

1 tablespoon hot sauce (I prefer Cholula)

1 teaspoon ground cumin

½ teaspoon kosher salt

½ teaspoon freshly ground black pepper

3 cups coleslaw mix or thinly sliced cabbage

½ cup finely chopped fresh cilantro leaves

TACOS

4 tablespoons avocado oil

1½ pounds oyster or portobello mushrooms, roughly chopped into bite-size pieces

3 tablespoons Taco Seasoning (recipe follows)

½ lime

4 large tortillas (I prefer 10-inch Siete Almond Flour Tortillas) or 8 small tortillas

Fresh cilantro leaves and lime wedges, for garnish

Tacos are, and forever will be, my jam, and these veggie-heavy babies are one of my faves when I'm in the mood for something nourishing, filling, and flavor-packed. The mushrooms get super crispy in the hot pan and pack a nice kick with my bespoke taco seasoning. They're topped with a cool and crunchy slaw, which is also great for many of the other bowls and tacos recipes in the book, grilled meat, fish, or veg, and definitely for my Dad's Oven-Baked Jammy Ribs (page 177).

Make the cilantro-lime slaw: In a large bowl, whisk together the yogurt, lime juice, hot sauce, 2 tablespoons water, cumin, salt, and pepper. The consistency should be similar to ranch dressing, so add more water if necessary. Add the coleslaw mix and cilantro, toss, and set aside.

Make the tacos: Heat 2 tablespoons of the avocado oil (or enough to fully coat the bottom) in a large skillet over medium heat until almost sizzling. Add half of the mushrooms without overcrowding (you want to cook in batches so the mushrooms don't steam) and cook, stirring occasionally but not too often, as you want them to spend some time sitting still in the pan to crisp up, about 3 minutes. Don't rush it! They need to get nice and crispy. Sprinkle in half of the taco seasoning and cook until the mushrooms are completely crispy, about 1 minute. Transfer to a plate. Repeat the process with the remaining oil, mushrooms, and seasoning. Squeeze the lime half over the mushrooms and stir to combine.

Heat the tortillas in the microwave or in a pan on the stovetop, transfer to a platter or individual plates, top with the mushrooms and slaw, and garnish with cilantro leaves and lime wedges.

Taco Seasoning

MAKES ABOUT ½ CUP

¼ cup chili powder

4 teaspoons ground cumin

4 teaspoons garlic powder

2 teaspoons onion powder

2 teaspoons sweet paprika

2 teaspoons kosher salt

1 teaspoon dried oregano

1 teaspoon freshly ground black pepper

½ to ¾ teaspoon cayenne pepper, to taste

In a small bowl, whisk together the chili powder, cumin, garlic powder, onion powder, paprika, salt, oregano, pepper, and cayenne. Transfer to a spice jar and store in the pantry.

Chicken Satay and Kale Salad

SERVES 4 TO 6 / TOTAL TIME: 40 MINUTES, PLUS 30 MINUTES (OR UP TO OVERNIGHT) MARINATING TIME
SPECIAL EQUIPMENT: 6 TO 8 BAMBOO OR METAL SKEWERS, OPTIONAL

MARINATED CHICKEN

1½ pounds boneless, skinless chicken breasts or thighs, cut into bite-size pieces

3 tablespoons reduced-sodium soy sauce

1 tablespoon toasted sesame oil

1 teaspoon grated and peeled fresh ginger

1 teaspoon sriracha

½ teaspoon ground turmeric

½ teaspoon freshly ground black pepper

KALE SALAD

6 tablespoons Peanut Ginger Dressing (recipe follows)

1 bunch curly kale, stems and ribs removed, leaves chopped (about 4 cups)

1 red bell pepper, diced

½ cucumber, peeled and diced

⅓ cup roasted salted peanuts, chopped

3 tablespoons chopped green onion

3 tablespoons finely chopped fresh mint leaves, plus more for garnish, optional

I'm an adventurous orderer, except when it comes to Thai food. I *always* order chicken satay as an app, and I *always* ask for at least two extra sides of peanut sauce to go with it. I like it so much I decided to come up with a way to eat it at home at least once a week, transforming it into a protein-packed chopped salad with kale, red pepper, cucumber, and (of course) more peanuts. If you want to go all-veggie, skip the chicken. I also double the dressing (surprise, surprise! lol) and keep it on hand to drizzle—okay, let's face it, drown—grilled shrimp, swordfish, grilled sliced steak, crudités, tofu . . . grain veggie bowls . . . you see where this is going . . .

Marinate the chicken: In a zip-seal plastic bag or large bowl, combine the chicken, soy sauce, sesame oil, ginger, sriracha, turmeric, and pepper and evenly distribute the marinade. Refrigerate for 30 minutes or overnight.

Preheat the oven to 425°F. Line a sheet pan with parchment paper.

Thread 5 or 6 pieces of chicken on each skewer and place on the sheet pan. (Alternatively, just place the chicken on the sheet pan by itself, but, like, what fun is that?) Bake until chicken is cooked through, 15 to 20 minutes.

Meanwhile, prep the kale salad: Make the Peanut Ginger Dressing (and try not to eat it all before the chicken is cooked).

To serve, in a large bowl, combine the kale, bell pepper, cucumber, peanuts, green onion, and mint. Add the dressing and toss until evenly combined. Divide into individual large shallow bowls or plates and top the salad with the chicken skewers and garnish with more fresh herbs if desired.

NOTES

Do not dress the salad until right before serving or the salad will wilt. If making both ahead, store the salad and dressing separately in the fridge.

In a pinch? Sub shredded rotisserie chicken for the chicken skewers!

Peanut Ginger Dressing

MAKES ABOUT ¼ CUP

3 tablespoons olive oil

3 tablespoons peanut butter

3 tablespoons reduced-sodium soy sauce

1 tablespoon honey

1 tablespoon toasted sesame oil

1 tablespoon rice vinegar

Juice of ½ lime

2 teaspoons fresh ginger, peeled and grated

1 garlic clove, finely chopped

In a food processor or blender, combine the olive oil, peanut butter, soy sauce, honey, sesame oil, vinegar, lime juice, ginger, and garlic and pulse until you have a smooth dressing, 1 to 2 minutes.

Arugula Salad with Creamy White Beans and Basil Vinaigrette

SERVES 4 / TOTAL TIME: 20 MINUTES

BASIL VINAIGRETTE

1 cup loosely packed fresh basil leaves

⅓ cup extra-virgin olive oil

1 tablespoon balsamic vinegar

1 tablespoon honey

1 teaspoon Dijon mustard

1 garlic clove, roughly chopped

Juice of 1 lemon

½ teaspoon kosher salt

¼ teaspoon freshly ground black pepper

SOURDOUGH CROUTONS

2½ tablespoons extra-virgin olive oil

2 cups sourdough bread, day-old, torn into ½-inch pieces

1 teaspoon kosher salt

1 teaspoon garlic powder

½ teaspoon freshly ground black pepper

CREAMY WHITE BEANS

2 tablespoons extra-virgin olive oil

2 (15-ounce) cans Great Northern beans, drained and rinsed

¼ teaspoon kosher salt, or more to taste

¼ teaspoon freshly ground black pepper

½ cup vegetable broth

2 tablespoons grated Parmesan cheese

SALAD

5 cups baby arugula

1 cup halved cherry tomatoes

Parmesan cheese shavings to top

Back when I was working my nine-to-five job in real estate, I used to get a salad for lunch at a restaurant down the street. It was about sixteen dollars, so it was a treat I could only really afford when my boss was paying. I loved the warm, creamy white beans with the slightly bitter and tangy arugula salad. Canned white beans are so hearty that you never feel like you're missing the meat in your meal! The heat from the creamy beans wilts the salad greens slightly, helping the flavor and textures come together. I highly recommend memorizing the basil vinaigrette recipe; it always finds its way last minute into many of the salads I make. And for a unique dip, try serving the creamy white beans solo with some potato chips to dip.

Make the dressing: In a food processor or blender, combine the basil, oil, vinegar, honey, mustard, garlic, lemon juice, salt, and pepper and pulse until the dressing is smooth and emulsified, about 1 minute.

Make the croutons: Heat the olive oil in a large skillet over medium heat. Add the bread, salt, garlic powder, and pepper and cook, stirring occasionally, until golden brown and crisp, about 5 minutes. Set aside.

Make the creamy white beans: Heat the olive oil in a large skillet over medium heat. Add the beans, season with the salt and pepper, and stir to combine. (Some canned beans are very salty, some come unsalted, so make sure to taste before seasoning!) Add the vegetable broth, bring to a simmer, and cook, stirring occasionally, until most of the liquid is absorbed, 2 to 3 minutes. Remove the pan from the heat and stir in the Parmesan.

Toss the arugula and tomatoes with ¾ of the vinaigrette. Divide the salad among 4 plates and serve with the creamy white beans, croutons, and Parmesan shavings on top. I'm a vinaigrette addict so I like to have extra on the side; you may not need it!

Shaved Brussels Sprouts Salad with Parmesan and Grapes

SERVES 4 / TOTAL TIME: 20 MINUTES

⅓ cup extra-virgin olive oil

Juice of 1 lemon

1½ tablespoons white wine vinegar

1½ teaspoons Dijon mustard

1 teaspoon maple syrup

¾ teaspoon kosher salt

¼ teaspoon freshly ground black pepper, or to taste

6 cups thinly shaved brussels sprouts (about one pound whole) (see Note), or 10 ounces store-bought shredded

½ cup pine nuts

1 cup red seedless grapes, halved

½ cup grated Parmesan cheese

NOTE

You can find already shaved brussels sprouts in most produce departments. Or, do what I do and Zen out while thinly slicing whole sprouts with a favorite playlist (see page 7) or a podcast for company!

This shaved brussels sprouts salad is one of my all-time favorites—pretty good for someone who "doesn't like brussels sprouts"! What works to counteract years of sad sprouts is that these are super thinly shaved raw so they're crisp but light and fluffy, ready to absorb the tart lemon vinaigrette and grated Parm. It's inspired by two of my favorite restaurants in LA, Elephante and Scopa. They both have incredible brussels sprouts salads that I have been personally asked by my Broccolinis to re-create on multiple occasions, so here you have it! Round it out with grilled chicken or shrimp for a Major Main or as a yummy side for a light lunch.

In a large bowl, whisk together the oil, lemon juice, vinegar, mustard, maple syrup, salt, and pepper. Add the brussels sprouts and toss to thoroughly coat in the vinaigrette. Let sit until the sprouts begin to soften, about 10 minutes.

Meanwhile, heat a small pan over medium-high heat until hot. Add the pine nuts and toast, stirring occasionally, until golden brown and fragrant, about 1 minute.

Stir the toasted pine nuts, grapes, and Parmesan into the brussels sprouts and toss to combine.

One-Pot Chipotle Chicken and Rice

SERVES 4 / TOTAL TIME: 30 MINUTES

SPICE MIX

2 teaspoons chili powder

2 teaspoons sweet paprika

1 teaspoon garlic powder

½ teaspoon dried oregano

1 teaspoon kosher salt

½ teaspoon freshly ground black pepper

CHICKEN AND RICE

1½ pounds boneless, skinless chicken thighs

4 to 6 tablespoons extra-virgin olive oil

1 yellow onion, diced

2 garlic cloves, finely chopped

1 chipotle pepper in adobo sauce

3 tablespoons honey

1 cup uncooked jasmine rice

2½ cups chicken broth

2 cups chopped curly kale leaves, ribs removed

3 tablespoons finely chopped fresh cilantro, for garnish

The problem with comfort food is that it doesn't just magically appear when you're craving it. Unless you're at your mom's house, you might have to make it yourself, which seems to defeat the point. That's why a really simple, warming dish like this is so important to have in your rep, delivering coziness on call without a lot of cleanup. Here, chicken and rice, that comfort juggernaut, gets another layer of deep heat from chipotles in adobo sauce that is balanced by the sweetness of the honey. Chipotle peppers are jalapeños that have been dried and smoked and are often sold packed in a sauce made from more chiles, dried herbs, and vinegar. There should always be a can in your pantry like there's always one in mine (see Grocery Run, page 11), but know that a little goes a loooong way. I had to learn that one the hard way. Once you open the can of chipotles in adobo, store the rest, tightly sealed, in the fridge for up to 2 weeks, or in the freezer for up to 3 months. For the greens in the dish, you can swap out the kale for collards, Swiss chard, spinach—whatever you like. And if you prefer things a little more brothy, add a little extra hot chicken broth to the pot for just the last 5 minutes so the rice still comes out perfect. This is beyond when you drizzle the creamy cilantro lime sauce from the Sheet Pan Blackened Salmon Bites with Potatoes, Broccoli, and Creamy Cilantro Sauce (page 76).

Make the spice mix: In a small bowl, stir together the chili powder, paprika, garlic powder, oregano, salt, and pepper to combine.

Make the chicken and rice: Season both sides of the chicken thighs with the spice mixture.

Heat a Dutch oven or large deep skillet with a lid over medium heat. Add 2 tablespoons of olive oil to the pot. Working in batches, sear the chicken thighs until they are golden brown but not fully cooked, 2 to 3 minutes per side. Place the seared thighs on a plate. Continue to sear the remaining chicken, adding oil to the pan as needed.

When all the chicken is cooked, add any additional oil needed to coat the bottom of your pan (about 2 tablespoons if the pan is dry) and heat over medium heat. Add the onion and garlic and cook, stirring occasionally, until softened, about 4 minutes. Add the chipotle pepper and honey and break up the pepper with a wooden spoon. Add the rice and stir to coat in the mixture. Add the

chicken broth and bring the mixture to a boil. Stir in the kale and arrange the chicken thighs on top. Reduce the heat to a simmer, cover, and cook until the rice is cooked, about 15 minutes.

Transfer to a serving plate and garnish with the cilantro.

Cheesy Sweet Potato Taco Bowls

SERVES 4 / TOTAL TIME: 30 MINUTES

CHEESY SWEET POTATOES

2 medium sweet potatoes, cut into ⅓- to ½-inch cubes

2 tablespoons avocado oil

2 tablespoons Taco Seasoning (page 97)

½ cup shredded Mexican blend cheese

CREAMY TACO SAUCE

½ cup whole-milk Greek yogurt

1 tablespoon Taco Seasoning (page 97)

Juice of 1 lime

2 teaspoons hot sauce (I prefer Cholula)

¼ teaspoon kosher salt

TACO BOWLS

4 cups Perfect Stovetop Rice (page 84), or cooked brown rice, for serving

1 (15-ounce) can black beans, drained and rinsed

2 ripe Roma or plum tomatoes, diced

1 avocado, cubed

1 jalapeño, sliced

3 tablespoons finely chopped fresh cilantro, for garnish

As a SoCal girl and big fan of Mexico, a large percentage of my food cravings can only be satisfied by something with culinary origins south of the border. Even better when it takes the form of a light and easy-to-make meal that's miraculously meatless. Meatless meals are often part of my mental and physical self-care routine, and this recipe delivers every time—vegetarian, yet packed with protein and—oh so satisfying. I'm personally a superfan of superfood sweet potatoes, but russets or Yukon Golds are always great, too, and a fine substitute. I mean, they're cheesy potato taco bowls, and there's just nothing wrong with that sentence at all. The creamy taco sauce is another one of my patented (wink) "make it for this recipe but use it to make a million other things more delicious" add-ons you'll reach for again and again. Bowls, tacos, enchiladas—even rescuing plain fried eggs on the days you've got an empty fridge and stomach!

Make the cheesy sweet potatoes: Preheat the oven to 400°F.

Add the sweet potato cubes to a large sheet pan. Sprinkle with the avocado oil and taco seasoning and toss to evenly coat. Bake until the sweet potatoes are soft on the inside and crispy on the outside, 16 to 20 minutes, tossing halfway through. Remove the pan from the oven, top the potatoes with the cheese, and return the pan to the oven for 30 seconds to 1 minute to melt the cheese.

Make the creamy taco sauce: In a small bowl, whisk together the yogurt, taco seasoning, lime juice, hot sauce, and ¼ teaspoon kosher salt. Taste and add more salt if needed.

Assemble the taco bowls: Add 1 cup of rice to the bottom of 4 bowls. Top with the cheesy sweet potatoes, black beans, tomatoes, avocado, and jalapeño. Top with cilantro and a generous drizzle of creamy taco sauce.

Roasted Fish with Sizzling Green Onion, Shallot, and Garlic Oil

SERVES 4 / TOTAL TIME: 20 MINUTES

4 fish fillets (6 ounces each), such as salmon or cod (skin on or off is your preference)

1 teaspoon kosher salt

Freshly ground black pepper

⅓ cup extra-virgin olive oil

1 large shallot, thinly sliced

2 garlic cloves, thinly sliced

3 green onions, thinly sliced on an angle

½ lemon, plus additional wedges, for serving

This recipe enhances the flavor of any familiar piece of fish. It's chic simplicity but also seriously impressive. I usually use salmon or cod because they're the freshest at my local grocery store, but talk to your fish seller or see what looks good to you. Arctic char (which tastes like a cross between a trout and milder salmon and is usually cheaper than either) and sole or flounder are also nice mild fish that really allow the other flavors in the dish to shine. The baking time will vary depending on the fish's thickness, so keep an eye on it while it cooks so you don't take it too far. To check doneness, use the thin tip of your knife to pierce the center of the fish and take a look. The flesh will be opaque when fully cooked. Just remember that it will continue to cook a bit out of the oven, especially when the hot oil sizzles on top. Serve this with Perfect Stovetop Rice (page 84) to catch all the garlicky-oniony oil.

Preheat the oven to 450°F. Line a sheet pan with parchment paper.

Place the fish on the lined sheet pan and season with the salt and ¼ teaspoon black pepper. Bake until the fish is opaque, 10 to 12 minutes. (Or if using salmon and you prefer it on the rarer side, check after 7 minutes—the salmon should be bright pink in the center and paler around the edges.)

Meanwhile, heat the olive oil in a small skillet or saucepan over medium heat. Once the oil is almost sizzling, add the shallot, garlic, and green onions and cook, stirring occasionally, until crispy, about 3 minutes. Reduce the heat if necessary, so it doesn't burn.

Transfer the fish to plates and top with the sizzling oil. Add a squeeze of fresh lemon juice and a few twists of pepper.

Turmeric Ginger Grain Bowls with Lemon-Tahini Sauce

SERVES 4 / TOTAL TIME: 30 MINUTES

ROASTED CHICKPEAS AND VEGETABLES

1 (15-ounce) can chickpeas, drained and rinsed

2 cups broccoli florets

1 red bell pepper, thinly sliced

1 red onion, thinly sliced

2 tablespoons extra-virgin olive oil

2 teaspoons ground turmeric

1 teaspoon garlic powder

1 teaspoon ground ginger

1 teaspoon kosher salt

½ teaspoon freshly ground black pepper

LEMON-TAHINI SAUCE

¼ cup tahini

1 garlic clove, finely chopped

Juice of 1 lemon

1 teaspoon maple syrup

¾ teaspoon kosher salt

¼ teaspoon cayenne pepper

2 tablespoons to ⅓ cup hot water

BOWLS

2 cups cooked quinoa, cooked according to package directions

1 avocado, thinly sliced

3 tablespoons crumbled feta cheese

In this book there are meals you make for a Saturday-night dinner party and meals you make after a weekend full of dinner parties. This meal is for the latter of those two scenarios, capable of bringing you back to life and getting you centered again. I created this recipe after my sister Amanda's wedding weekend, a crazy-fun couple of days filled with rich food washed down with a lot of tequila and champagne. We all have our moments, okay? The protein boost from the quinoa, chickpeas, and tahini combined with the anti-inflammatory properties of the turmeric and the well-documented restorative power of ginger and garlic was just the trick to getting me back on my A game. This recipe is my secret weapon and will get you feeling like a functioning adult once again, or whenever you need a boost!

Roast the chickpeas and vegetables: Preheat the oven to 400°F.

In a large bowl, toss together the chickpeas, broccoli, bell pepper, and onion. Add the olive oil and sprinkle with the turmeric, garlic powder, ground ginger, salt, and pepper and toss to coat.

Spread out on a sheet pan and bake until the chickpeas are golden brown and the veggies are browned and tender when pierced with a fork, 15 to 20 minutes, tossing halfway through.

Meanwhile, make the lemon-tahini sauce: In a blender, combine the tahini, garlic, lemon juice, maple syrup, salt, and cayenne. With the blender running, slowly drizzle in enough hot water until the sauce has the consistency of a vinaigrette.

Assemble the bowls: Scoop ½ cup quinoa into each of 4 bowls. Dividing evenly, top with the roasted chickpeas and vegetables, avocado, and feta. Drizzle with the lemon-tahini sauce.

Pistachio Pesto Salmon

SERVES 2 / TOTAL TIME: 20 MINUTES

¼ cup salted roasted pistachios (if using unsalted, increase salt by ¼ teaspoon)

2 cups packed fresh basil leaves

¼ cup grated Parmesan cheese

1 garlic clove, roughly chopped

½ teaspoon kosher salt

Freshly ground black pepper

Juice of ½ lemon, or more to taste

½ cup extra-virgin olive oil, plus more if needed

2 salmon fillets (6 ounces each) (skin on or off is your preference)

Lemon wedges, for squeezing

It's incredible how family, food, and social media have evolved and changed my life. Back in 2017 when I had an idea to start documenting my meals, I decided to start with this one. I still cringe when I look at the photo I posted back then. Luckily, my photography skills have come a long way! This is one of my favorite things my mom makes and I'm so grateful to be able to share it and hope it becomes your favorite, too! I've always been a huge pistachio girl, so adding them to some pesto and slathering it all over my favorite fish is just the ultimate. Here's another case where I can't get enough of the sauce, so I often double the batch of pesto and add it to everything from pasta to sandwiches—you name it! Even though store-bought shelled pistachios are easier to work with, it's one of life's greatest pleasures to be cooking while shelling and snacking on them. It gives you a moment to think about what else this pesto will rock, like a swordfish steak or plump chicken breast. Feel free to throw some broccoli or asparagus on the sheet pan with the salmon, as they both call for the same cooking time.

Preheat the oven to 400°F. Line a sheet pan with foil.

Make the pistachio pesto: In a food processor, combine the pistachios, basil, Parmesan, garlic, salt, a few twists of pepper, lemon juice, and 2 tablespoons of the olive oil and pulse 3 to 4 times. While the machine is running, slowly drizzle in the remaining oil for about 30 seconds. The pesto should have a little texture and not be too oily. If it appears dry, transfer it to a small bowl, and stir in more oil, 1 tablespoon at a time, until the mixture is easily spreadable and moist.

Cook the salmon: Set the salmon on the sheet pan. Generously coat the top of the salmon with the pesto and bake until the salmon is opaque in the center, 10 to 12 minutes. If you prefer your fish on the rare side, it will be closer to 9 to 10 minutes and the flesh will be bright pink in the center and slightly translucent.

To serve: Transfer the fish to a platter, or 2 individual plates, and add lemon wedges for squeezing.

Sun-Dried Tomato and Feta Turkey Burgers with Jalapeño Tzatziki

SERVES 4 / TOTAL TIME: 30 MINUTES

JALAPEÑO TZATZIKI

½ cucumber

¾ cup whole-milk Greek yogurt

1 tablespoon extra-virgin olive oil

1 tablespoon diced jalapeño (seeded if you want less heat)

1 tablespoon chopped fresh dill

1 tablespoon chopped fresh mint

Juice of ½ lemon

1 garlic clove, finely chopped

½ teaspoon kosher salt

TURKEY BURGERS

1 cup baby spinach, roughly chopped

1 pound lean ground turkey

⅓ cup oil-packed sun-dried tomatoes, drained and finely chopped

⅓ cup crumbled feta cheese

¼ red onion, diced

1 garlic clove, finely chopped

1 teaspoon dried oregano

1 teaspoon dried parsley

½ teaspoon kosher salt

½ teaspoon freshly ground black pepper

2 tablespoons extra-virgin olive oil

8 large Bibb or leaf lettuce leaves

This healthy twist on a gyro, seasoned with the classic Greek spinach/feta/oregano trio, is the juiciest turkey burger you've ever had thanks to the surprising addition of sun-dried tomatoes packed in olive oil. They're great served as a lettuce wrap if you want to go lighter or let it rock your world in a grilled pita or hamburger bun. If you don't have (or don't like) sun-dried tomatoes, replace them with green olives and a tablespoon of olive oil and cut the salt down to ¼ teaspoon. Also, don't toss the cucumber water left over from grating the cuke for your tzatziki: Add it to water and enjoy a refreshing spa drink or head in the other direction and stir it into a margarita! Your feel-good food list just got longer!

Make the jalapeño tzatziki: Over a sieve set in a bowl, grate the cucumber on the large holes of a box grater. Using a kitchen towel, fine-mesh sieve, or your hands, wring or press out any excess liquid from the cucumber.

In a medium bowl, combine the grated cucumber, yogurt, oil, jalapeño, dill, mint, lemon juice, garlic, and salt. Taste and adjust the seasoning, if needed. Cover with plastic wrap and refrigerate while you make the burgers. You can even make the tzatziki the night before (it tastes even better the next day!).

Make the turkey burgers: In a medium skillet, combine the spinach and 2 tablespoons of water and cook over medium heat, stirring frequently, until wilted, about 1 minute. Remove and allow to cool slightly.

In a large bowl, combine the wilted spinach, turkey, sun-dried tomatoes, feta, onion, garlic, oregano, parsley, salt, and pepper and gently mix to evenly distribute all the ingredients. Divide the mixture into 4 equal portions and form them into patties about 1-inch thick, slightly indenting the middle of each patty with your thumb. (The indentation helps the patty stay nice and flat instead of puffing up like a football.)

Heat the olive oil in a large skillet over medium-high heat. Add the patties and cook until browned and cooked through, about 8 minutes per side (or when an instant meat thermometer inserted horizontally reads 165°F).

Top the patty with a generous dollop of tzatziki and wrap each burger in 2 lettuce leaves per burger.

Coconut Green Curry Shrimp

SERVES 4 / TOTAL TIME: 30 MINUTES

2 tablespoons coconut oil

1½ pounds large shrimp, peeled and deveined, tails removed

½ teaspoon kosher salt

½ teaspoon freshly ground black pepper

1 yellow onion, thinly sliced into half-moons

1 green bell pepper, halved lengthwise and thinly sliced crosswise

1 jalapeño, chopped

1 tablespoon grated and peeled fresh ginger (from about a 3-inch piece)

2 garlic cloves, finely chopped

2 tablespoons Thai green curry paste

2 tablespoons fish sauce

1 tablespoon reduced-sodium soy sauce

1½ teaspoons light brown sugar

1 (13½-ounce) can full-fat coconut milk

Grated zest and juice of 1 lime

1 cup fresh basil leaves, thinly sliced

4 cups cooked Perfect Stovetop Rice (page 84), for serving

3 tablespoons finely chopped fresh cilantro, for garnish

Of all the Thai curries, I prefer the bright, fragrant lemongrass flavor of a green curry. It's a snap to make at home when you keep a good-quality store-bought Thai curry paste in the fridge. Shrimp is my favorite protein with curry, but you can swap it out for salmon, chicken, beef, or even tofu. This recipe is incredibly versatile, so have fun with it! It's a nourishing, comforting weeknight dinner when you're feeling the need for some spice in your life. The recipe scales up easily by doubling or even tripling, and to lay the groundwork for a simple future meal, I'll often make just the sauce and freeze it. Then I thaw the sauce the night before I want to use it, heat it up, cook the shrimp as directed, add the sauce to the shrimp, and simmer for 1 minute. Curry in a hurry!

Heat 1 tablespoon of the coconut oil in a large Dutch oven or large pot over medium heat. Add the shrimp in an even layer and season with the salt and pepper. Cook until just cooked through, about 2 minutes on each side. Transfer the shrimp to a plate and set aside.

Add the remaining 1 tablespoon coconut oil to the pan. Add the onion, bell pepper, jalapeño, ginger, and garlic and cook, stirring occasionally, until the onion is translucent, 6 to 8 minutes.

Add the curry paste and stir to combine. Stir in the fish sauce, soy sauce, brown sugar, and coconut milk and bring the curry to a simmer.

Return the shrimp to the pan and stir in the lime zest, lime juice, and basil.

Serve the curry over rice and garnish with the cilantro.

Turkey and Sweet Potato Skillet

SERVES 4 / TOTAL TIME: 35 MINUTES

2 tablespoons extra-virgin olive oil or avocado oil

1 yellow onion, diced

2 garlic cloves, finely chopped

1 pound ground turkey

1 tablespoon chili powder

1½ teaspoons ground cumin

1½ teaspoons garlic powder

Kosher salt

Freshly ground black pepper

2 cups roughly chopped broccoli florets

1 red bell pepper, diced

1 large sweet potato, peeled and cut into ½- to ¾-inch cubes

¾ cup water, chicken broth, or vegetable broth

½ cup shredded mozzarella or Mexican blend cheese

Whole-milk Greek yogurt or sour cream, for serving

Chopped fresh cilantro, for garnish

Thinly sliced green onion, for garnish

Hot sauce for serving, optional

This is an OG recipe, a blog favorite that I created back in 2018 when I was just a little baby Brocc! Many of my followers (I love you, Broccolinis!) have told me it's one of their weekly staples, so I'd be crazy not to include it in the book. This recipe is great if you're looking for a new way to use ground turkey. It's also a terrific veggie bin clear-out recipe, as it's VERY flexible and forgiving if you want to make a few swaps here and there. A regular russet or Yukon Gold for the sweet potato? No problem! Zucchini in place of the broccoli? Go for it! It's fun to serve this straight from the skillet, but please don't skip the cilantro and green onion garnish—they add a fresh herbal brightness that will help put this dish in your weekly rotation, too!

Heat the olive oil in a large skillet over medium heat. Once hot, add the onion and garlic and cook, stirring occasionally, until fragrant, 2 to 3 minutes. Increase the heat to medium-high. Add the turkey and cook, without stirring, until lightly browned, about 2 minutes. Continue to cook, stirring frequently and breaking the meat up with a wooden spoon, until browned all over, about 3 minutes. Add the chili powder, cumin, garlic powder, 1 teaspoon kosher salt, and ¼ teaspoon pepper and stir to thoroughly combine.

Add the broccoli, bell pepper, sweet potato, and water and stir to combine. Reduce the heat to low, cover, and simmer until the sweet potatoes are tender when pierced with a fork and the water is absorbed, 15 to 20 minutes. Taste and season with more salt and/or pepper. Add the cheese, cover, and cook until the cheese melts, about 1 minute.

Serve right out of the skillet or divide among 4 bowls. Top with the yogurt, cilantro, and green onion. Pass hot sauce at the table for anyone who wants it.

Kofta (Spiced Meatballs) and Shirazi Salad

SERVES 4 / TOTAL TIME: 25 MINUTES

My mom and I are crazy for Mediterranean food and end up eating it almost every time we have lunch together. No complaints from me! I love the fresh flavors and zip that Middle Eastern spices offer kebabs, but I thought kofta were a fun spin and actually way easier than dealing with skewers and making kebabs. It's a fast recipe, jam-packed with flavor and bright ingredients that are easy to find—with the exception of sumac, which you may have to order online; it adds a lovely tartness, but you can use lime juice in its place. I also love stuffing an open pita with some meatballs, salad, and drizzling with hot sauce and tahini for a delicious and filling lunch. It's a must-try. Shirazi salad is my take on a brightly flavored chopped salad with fresh herbs, cukes, tomatoes, onions, and, of course, EVOO, which you'll find all over the Eastern Mediterranean, and goes by different names depending on what country you're in. I think it's delicious in any language!

SHIRAZI SALAD

4 to 5 Persian (mini) cucumbers, small dice (about 2 cups)

2 large ripe Roma tomatoes, diced

½ red onion, diced

2 tablespoons finely chopped fresh basil

2 tablespoons finely chopped fresh mint

2 tablespoons finely chopped fresh parsley

3 tablespoons extra-virgin olive oil

Juice of 1 lime

1 teaspoon kosher salt

½ teaspoon sumac (or a pinch of chili powder and an extra squeeze of lime juice)

Freshly ground black pepper

MEATBALLS

1 small yellow onion, peeled and quartered

¾ cup fresh parsley

2 garlic cloves, peeled but whole

1 pound ground beef, 85% lean

1 teaspoon ground coriander

1 teaspoon ground cumin

1 teaspoon sweet paprika

½ teaspoon ground cinnamon

½ teaspoon ground ginger

½ teaspoon kosher salt

½ teaspoon freshly ground black pepper

2 tablespoons extra-virgin olive oil

FOR SERVING (OPTIONAL)

Pita bread

Tahini

Hot sauce

Make the shirazi salad: In a large bowl, toss to combine the cucumbers, tomatoes, red onion, basil, mint, and parsley. Drizzle on the oil and sprinkle with the lime juice, salt, and sumac (or a pinch of chili powder and an extra squeeze of lime). Toss to thoroughly coat. Taste and season with more salt and some pepper, if desired. Cover and refrigerate until ready to serve.

Make the meatballs: In a food processor, combine the yellow onion, parsley, and garlic and pulse for about 20 seconds, or until finely chopped and combined. Add the beef, coriander, cumin, paprika, cinnamon, ginger, salt, and pepper and process until thoroughly combined, about 30 seconds.

tablespoon to form the meat mixture into about 24 small balls.

Heat the olive oil in a cast-iron skillet or other large skillet over medium heat. Add the meatballs and cook, turning occasionally, until browned and cooked through, about 10 minutes. If

cooking in batches, add more oil as needed.

Serve the meatballs with the shirazi salad and pita bread. If desired, drizzle with some tahini and pass the hot sauce!

Or to make sandwiches, stuff 4 to 6 meatballs in a pita, divide the salad evenly among them, drizzle with tahini and hot sauce.

RESTAU-RANT REMAKES

Southern California has an eclectic mix of restaurants, from the classic Hollywood staples, to trendy hipster hangouts, to the West Side neighborhood restaurants I frequent so much that I don't even read the menu anymore. I've been pretty successful re-creating some of my favorite dishes throughout the years, and this chapter is my chance to share my takes on some personal menu favorites from my early years, college throwbacks, and even my all-time favorite pasta dish (from NYC, of course). And if you've been following me on IG, you know that I am no stranger to the occasional drive-thru meal—those irresistible fast-food runs we all go on from time to time (c'mon, admit it!). I've

also included "Broccified" (read: healthy) recipes for those mystery-ingredient take-out dishes, so now you can enjoy better-for-you versions of a "Fried" Chicken Sandwich with Special Sauce (page 132), my Chinese take-out favorite, Honey-Walnut Shrimp (page 135), and my Mom's Smashed Burgers with Mac Sauce (page 143).

If you're wondering how I sleuthed these recipes out, I chat up the waiters and ask a few pointed questions—it's a game rather than flat-out asking for the recipe. Half the fun is then trying to re-create it with my own spin back at home—and there's a little poetic license taken, too.

Famous Beverly Hills Chopped Salad

SERVES 6 / TOTAL TIME: 30 MINUTES, 1 HOUR TO MARINATE THE CHICKPEAS

DRESSING

¼ cup extra-virgin olive oil

2 tablespoons red wine vinegar

½ teaspoon Dijon mustard

1 clove garlic, finely chopped or crushed

½ teaspoon kosher salt

¼ teaspoon dried oregano

Freshly ground black pepper

SALAD

1 (15-ounce) can chickpeas, drained and rinsed

3 cups finely chopped romaine lettuce

3 cups finely chopped iceberg lettuce

3 ripe Roma tomatoes, diced

1 cucumber, diced

½ cup diced low-moisture mozzarella cheese

¼ cup grated Parmesan cheese, plus more for serving

3 ounces salami, chopped

2 tablespoons chopped fresh basil

Kosher salt, to taste

Freshly ground black pepper, to taste

Lemon wedges for squeezing

This recipe, more than any other, has gone the most viral on social media! It's a version of the chopped salad from the iconic Beverly Hills restaurant La Scala that's been serving Hollywood moguls since the 1950s. If there's such a thing as a celeb salad this is probably it, with everyone from President Kennedy to the Kardashians said to be fans. It's the best parts of an Italian hero, and you may have all the ingredients on hand, especially if you keep a hard salami in your fridge bin like I do! If you don't have fresh basil, try the same amount of fresh parsley or a teaspoon of dried oregano. There's no right or wrong when it comes to the La Scala salad.

Make the dressing: In a small bowl, whisk together the oil, vinegar, mustard, garlic, salt, oregano, and a few twists of pepper. Set aside.

In a small bowl, toss the chickpeas in 2 tablespoons of the dressing. Refrigerate for at least 1 hour.

In a large serving bowl, combine the romaine, iceberg, tomatoes, cucumber, mozzarella, Parmesan, salami, basil, salt, and pepper. Add the refrigerated chickpeas and the remaining dressing and toss to evenly combine. Serve with lemon wedges for squeezing and more grated Parmesan.

Hibachi-Style Fried Rice with Ginger Sauce

SERVES 4 / TOTAL TIME: 20 MINUTES

GINGER SAUCE

¼ yellow onion, peeled and quartered

1½-inch piece fresh ginger, peeled and roughly chopped

⅓ cup reduced-sodium soy sauce

1½ tablespoons rice vinegar

Juice of ½ lemon

1 tablespoon coconut or light brown sugar

GARLIC BUTTER

1 stick (4 ounces) unsalted butter, at room temperature

4 garlic cloves, finely chopped

3 tablespoons reduced-sodium soy sauce

FRIED RICE

3 tablespoons avocado oil

2 carrots, peeled and chopped

½ yellow onion, chopped

4 cups Perfect Stovetop Rice, (page 84), preferably day-old

1 pound small shrimp, peeled and deveined, tails removed

3 large eggs, beaten

2 tablespoons sesame seeds

¼ cup green onions, thinly sliced

Let's be real here . . . the reason I'm going to Benihana is for the flaming onion volcano and the little bowl of tasty fried rice they serve before dinner that I instantly devour. Although I haven't mastered the onion volcano (yet), the hibachi-style fried rice recipe has officially been nailed. Personally, I douse my rice in that ginger sauce they serve because it is just so damn good, so needless to say that recipe is included here as well. You can put it on just about everything, but it makes a particularly delicious dressing for salads. Couple of crucial tricks for fried rice: Always use day-old rice! Freshly cooked rice equals soggy fried rice equals sad, gummy dinner. Second tip, clear a space for those scrambled eggs, make sure the pan is really hot, and add a touch more oil before you crack in the eggs. Using a chopstick creates the perfect scrambled curds, and will get you into those authentic Benihana vibes. Omit the protein and level-up on the veggies if that's your thing. And don't worry, you can still put on a show: just flambé the Bananas Foster (page 255) for a grand finale!

Make the ginger sauce: In a blender or food processor, combine the onion, ginger, soy sauce, vinegar, lemon juice, and sugar and blend until smooth, about 1 minute. Set aside.

Make the garlic butter: In a small bowl, mix together the butter, garlic, and soy sauce until smooth.

Fry the rice: Heat 2 tablespoons of the avocado oil in a large skillet over medium heat. Add the carrots and onion and cook, stirring, until slightly softened, 3 to 4 minutes. Increase the heat to medium-high, add the rice, shrimp, and garlic butter, and cook until the rice is crispy and the shrimp are opaque throughout, about 4 minutes.

Push the rice mixture to one side and add the remaining 1 tablespoon of oil to the space. Once the oil is hot, add the eggs and use a chopstick or fork to quickly scramble the eggs. Remove the pan from the heat, mix the eggs with the rice mixture, stir in the sesame seeds and green onions, and serve with the ginger sauce on the side.

Prosciutto and Parmesan Tagliatelle

SERVES 4 / TOTAL TIME: 20 MINUTES

2 tablespoons kosher salt for pasta water

1 pound tagliatelle (preferably fresh but I get it if that's not in the cards)

6 tablespoons unsalted butter

2 garlic cloves, finely chopped

⅓ cup heavy cream

¾ cup grated Parmigiano-Reggiano cheese

Kosher salt

Freshly ground black pepper

5 ounces sliced prosciutto, thinly sliced

Freshly shaved Parmigiano-Reggiano, for garnish

The Tagliatelle from Via Carota in New York City shifted my entire state of being. I would make the trip across the country just for that. There's really nothing over the top about it, just simply delicious and clearly made with some seriously high-quality ingredients. They take tagliatelle, coat it in some insane cream sauce, and top it with thinly sliced salty prosciutto and tons of fresh Parmesan cheese, the authentic one labeled Parmigiano-Reggiano. The difference is Parmigiano-Reggiano is actually regulated and comes from a specific region in Italy, must be aged for at least one year, and has a distinctive, slightly sharp, fruity, and nutty taste that is really worth the extra dough for this recipe. It is nothing short of heaven. The remake recipe is going to be as good as the ingredients you buy, so don't skimp here! Especially with the prosciutto and Parmesan. A trip to your local Italian market will be well worth it. You can also make it a project by making your own pasta, or if you're not friendly with dough like I am, just venture to Eataly or your favorite Italian market. For the classic New York sweet finish try my version of the Italian trattoria Maialino's Rosemary Almond Orange Olive Oil Cake (page 252).

Bring a pot of salted water to a boil. Add the tagliatelle and cook to al dente according to the package directions. Reserve 1 cup of the pasta water, drain the pasta.

When the pasta is about 2 minutes away from being done, melt the butter in a large skillet over medium heat. Once it has just melted, add the garlic and cook, stirring frequently, until fragrant and slightly soft, about 45 seconds. Increase the heat to medium-high, add the heavy cream, and bring to a simmer.

Add the cooked pasta to the pan and slowly stir in the grated Parmesan. Add the reserved pasta water a few tablespoons at a time until the pasta is creamy and smooth (you may not need more than ½ cup). Season with salt and pepper to taste.

Divide the pasta among individual bowls and top with prosciutto slices and tons of freshly shaved Parmigiano-Reggiano cheese.

NOTE

I use a Microplane to shave the cheese over the pasta for the garnish.

Mediterranean-Style Tuna Wrap

SERVES 4 / TOTAL TIME: 15 MINUTES

TUNA SALAD

4 (5-ounce) cans water-packed tuna, drained

¾ cup mayonnaise

1 celery stalk, finely chopped

3 tablespoons finely chopped red onion

3 tablespoons finely chopped pickled jalapeños, optional

Juice of ½ lemon

½ teaspoon kosher salt

¼ teaspoon freshly ground black pepper

GREEK DRESSING

¼ cup extra-virgin olive oil

Juice of ½ lemon

2 tablespoons red wine vinegar

½ teaspoon Dijon mustard

½ teaspoon dried oregano

¼ teaspoon kosher salt

¼ teaspoon freshly ground black pepper

SALAD

3 cups mixed greens or chopped romaine

1 ripe Roma tomato, diced

½ cup chopped cucumber

⅓ cup chopped pitted kalamata olives

⅓ cup crumbled feta cheese

⅓ cup roasted and salted pistachios, shelled

WRAPS

4 (10-inch) spinach tortillas

My sister, Amanda, lives an hour away, in Newport Beach. If I time it just right, she will have this tuna wrap from Jan's Health Bar waiting for me the minute I pull into her driveway. I honestly didn't even care for tuna until this wrap came into my life. My at-home remake has become a weekly lunch staple that I just can't get enough of. I often make a double batch of the recipe and keep the tuna salad, Greek salad, and dressing stored separately and throw the wraps together right before devouring them. The punch of the tuna and pickled jalapeño combo nestled together with the Greek salad is so satisfying and a real protein boost for when I'm feeling sluggish and need a pick-me-up.

Make the tuna salad: In a medium bowl, mix together the tuna, mayonnaise, celery, onion, jalapeños (if using), lemon juice, salt, and pepper. Set aside.

Make the dressing: In a small bowl, whisk together the olive oil, lemon juice, vinegar, mustard, oregano, salt, and pepper. (If making ahead, store this separately.)

Make the Greek salad: In a large bowl, toss together the greens, tomato, cucumber, olives, feta, and pistachios. Add the dressing and toss again to combine.

Divide the tuna evenly among the tortillas. Top with about 1 cup of salad. Wrap it up and serve.

"Fried" Chicken Sandwich with Special Sauce

SERVES 4 / TOTAL TIME: 35 MINUTES

SPECIAL SAUCE

1 cup mayonnaise

¼ cup BBQ sauce

¼ cup honey

¼ cup yellow mustard

1 tablespoon fresh lemon juice

CRISPY CHICKEN

2 cups almond flour

1 cup tapioca flour

1 teaspoon chili powder

1 teaspoon garlic powder

1 teaspoon kosher salt

1 teaspoon freshly ground black pepper

½ teaspoon cayenne pepper

2 large eggs

4 boneless, skinless chicken thighs (about 5 ounces each)

Avocado oil for shallow frying

SANDWICHES

4 brioche buns (or gluten-free buns for a completely GF recipe)

2 tablespoons unsalted butter, at room temperature

2 ripe beefsteak tomatoes, sliced

⅓ cup dill pickle chips

2 cups shredded lettuce

Pickled jalapeños, as many as you want!

There was absolutely no way I wasn't including these crispy chicken sandwiches in the book. It's one of my most prized recipes from the blog, and I know my readers are just as obsessed with it as I am because it's pretty much everything you want in a bite. If you ditch the bun for a lettuce wrap or use gluten-free buns, it's all grain-free. The incredible crunch comes from the almond and tapioca flours, so the chicken is light yet crispy, with just the right amount of garlic and heat from the spice mix. Add the tangy special sauce to a soft buttered, toasted bun piled high with tomatoes, pickles, and, if you want to go all in, the pickled jalapeños . . . game over. It tastes even better on a Sunday when Chick-fil-A is closed. My friends and I pack them up in foil to take to the beach or the park during summer. They hold up surprisingly well for a picnic, and taste ten times better after an ocean dip. I'm pretty sure that's the real reason they invite me to the beach.

Make the special sauce: In a small bowl, combine the mayo, BBQ sauce, honey, mustard, and lemon juice.

Make the crispy chicken: Line a large plate or sheet pan with paper towels.

Set up a breading station in 2 large shallow bowls. Combine the almond flour, tapioca flour, chili powder, garlic powder, salt, pepper, and cayenne in one bowl. Beat the eggs in a second bowl.

Place a chicken thigh between 2 pieces of plastic wrap and use a meat mallet, rolling pin, or even the bottom of a coffee cup to lightly pound the thighs to about ½-inch thickness. Repeat for all 4 thighs.

Coat the chicken in the beaten egg, then press into the almond flour mixture and place on a large plate.

Pour ¼ inch of the avocado oil into a large skillet over medium-high heat to between 350° and 370°F. To test the oil, either use an instant-read thermometer or drop in a bit of the almond flour mixture—it should sizzle and float to the top.

Working in batches, add the chicken thighs to the pan, reducing the heat if necessary. Cook until the chicken is crispy and cooked through, 3 to 5 minutes per side. (The cooking time will depend on how thinly you've pounded your chicken. It's okay to carefully remove a thigh and peek by

piercing the thickest part with a knife, because the dark meat is so moist.) Transfer the chicken to the paper towels and blot any excess oil.

Set a skillet over medium-high heat. Split the buns and spread the butter over both insides of the buns. Add the buns, buttered-side down, to the hot skillet and toast until golden brown and crispy, 1 to 2 minutes. Flip them over and toast the top part of the bun if you'd like. (Alternatively, you can do this under the broiler.)

Spread the sauce on the toasted buns, top with a piece of crispy chicken (cut them in half and overlap them if they're larger than the bun), and top with the tomatoes and pickles. And in violation of Chick-fil-A, add lettuce and pickled jalapeños.

Honey-Walnut Shrimp

SERVES 4 / TOTAL TIME: 30 MINUTES

CANDIED WALNUTS

Canola or other neutral oil for the sheet pan

⅓ cup coconut sugar or dark brown sugar

1 cup walnuts

Pinch of kosher salt

CRISPY SHRIMP

½ cup mayonnaise, preferably Kewpie

2 tablespoons honey

¾ cup cornstarch or tapioca flour

¼ teaspoon kosher salt

¼ teaspoon freshly ground black pepper

1 large egg

1 pound large shrimp (¹⁸/₂₀ count), peeled and deveined, tails on

3 tablespoons canola oil, or more as needed

FOR SERVING

1 cup shredded cabbage

3 cups Perfect Stovetop Rice (page 84)

I worked at a Chinese restaurant when I was in college and I think I gained a solid five pounds after discovering this dish on the menu. Oops! But by now, you know me well enough to realize my philosophy is not about beating myself up over things like that, it's more about moderation (which I've learned since then). The best part of this recipe is that you can kind of split the difference with my healthier remake of this otherwise decadent Honey-Walnut Shrimp. What's not to love about plump, crunchy shrimp topped with warm candied nuts? It's just the perfect combo! Biggest healthy makeover tip is the light dusting of cornstarch and egg that adds enough crispiness so you can shallow-fry instead of deep-frying, which means A LOT less oil (and cleanup) is needed! That crunch plays beautifully off the light coating of creamy mayo sauce and is made iconic when topped with sticky candied walnuts (which are also perfect for snacking on their own, btw!). If you're looking for a green veg to pair, steamed broccoli goes great with this one!

Make the candied walnuts: Line a sheet pan with parchment paper and lightly oil the parchment.

Heat a large nonstick skillet over medium heat. Add the coconut sugar and ⅓ cup of water and cook, stirring constantly until the sugar dissolves. Bring the mixture to a boil and stir in the walnuts and salt. Continue to cook, stirring frequently, until the water is fully evaporated, about 4 minutes. Remove from the heat and quickly scrape the walnuts into a smooth layer so they do not clump onto the prepared sheet pan. Set aside.

Make the crispy shrimp: In a large bowl, stir together the mayonnaise and honey. Set aside.

Set up a dredging station in 2 shallow bowls. Stir together the cornstarch, salt, and pepper in one bowl. In the second bowl, beat the egg. Add the shrimp to the beaten egg and toss to evenly coat. Coat the shrimp in the seasoned cornstarch and shake off any excess. Set the coated shrimp on a large plate while you heat the oil.

Heat 3 tablespoons canola oil in a large skillet over medium heat. When the oil is almost sizzling, add the shrimp in one layer. (You may need to do 2 batches.) Cook until golden brown on both sides, 2 to 3 minutes per side. Add more oil if you are frying a second batch.

To serve, add the crispy shrimp to the bowl with the mayonnaise mixture and toss to evenly coat. Place the shrimp on a bed of shredded cabbage, top with candied walnuts, and serve with rice.

Healthier Homemade Crunchy Burrito Wrap

SERVES 4 / TOTAL TIME: 30 MINUTES

TACO FILLING

1 tablespoon avocado oil

1 pound ground beef, 85% lean

1 tablespoon Taco Seasoning (page 97)

1 teaspoon tapioca flour or cornstarch

⅓ cup cold water

⅓ cup shredded Mexican blend cheese

8 (12-inch) burrito-size almond flour, or flour tortillas (I like Siete Foods tortillas)

4 (5-inch) tostadas, homemade (see Note) or store-bought

1 cup whole-milk Greek yogurt or sour cream

2 avocados, mashed

3 cups shredded lettuce

2 tomatoes, diced

1 tablespoon avocado oil

NOTE

I often make my own tostadas by frying the trimmed almond flour tortilla in some avocado oil in a skillet until it's crunchy on both sides. Or, instead of store-bought tostadas, you can split hard-shell tacos or even tortilla chips!

I feel like my brand was built off the back of my Taco Bell re-creations way back in 2017 when I first became "Brocc." My first viral recipe was my remake of their delicious and utterly craveable Crunchwrap Supreme. It put me on the IG map (thanks for the inspo, Taco Bell!) and I will forever be thought of as "The Crunchwrap Girl" by the Broccolinis who've come to cherish that dish. So here, we finally come full circle as I publish my original Crunchwrap replica in my very first cookbook. Now that's something to celebrate! This recipe still relies on all the best parts of the TB magic—creamy beans, gooey cheese, warm, soft tortillas, and that insane *crrrrrunch*—but with my Taco Seasoning (page 97), wholesome ingredients, and my fave almond flour tortillas for those signature Brocc Your Body vibes.

Make the taco filling: Heat the avocado oil in a large skillet over medium heat. Add the meat and cook, using a wooden spoon or meat masher to break the meat up, until the meat is almost fully browned, about 5 minutes. Stir in the taco seasoning and cook, stirring occasionally, until the meat is no longer pink and is fully browned. If you like a more "saucy" beef, whisk the tapioca flour or cornstarch with the cold water in a small bowl, and stir it into the meat, then simmer until the liquid dissolves, 3 to 5 minutes. Remove the meat from the heat and immediately stir in the shredded cheese until melted.

Assemble the wraps: Place 4 of the flour tortillas on a large cutting board. Place a tostada in the center of the tortilla and, using a scissor or a knife, trim the flour tortilla to be the same size as the tostada. Set aside.

Divide the beef filling among 4 of the untrimmed flour tortillas and top each with Greek yogurt (or sour cream). Place a tostada on top of the yogurt. Top with the avocado, lettuce, and tomatoes. Top with the smaller trimmed tortilla and gently fold the large tortilla to form a large burrito wrap.

Heat the avocado oil in a large nonstick skillet over medium-high heat. Add the wraps seam-side down and cook until golden brown and crisp on both sides, 1 to 2 minutes on each side. Slice in half and serve.

Honey Dijon Vinaigrette

MAKES ABOUT ¾ CUP

¼ cup olive oil

Juice of ½ lemon

2 tablespoons apple cider vinegar

2 teaspoons honey

1 teaspoon Dijon mustard

1 garlic clove, finely chopped

½ teaspoon kosher salt

⅛ teaspoon freshly ground black pepper

In a small bowl, whisk together the olive oil, lemon juice, vinegar, honey, mustard, garlic, salt, and pepper and set aside.

Venice Grain Bowls with 8-Minute Egg

SERVES 4 / TOTAL TIME: 30 MINUTES

1 cup uncooked sprouted brown rice (or 3 cups Perfect Stovetop Rice, page 84)

4 large eggs

4 cups mixed greens

1 carrot, peeled and shaved into strips

1 radish, thinly sliced

2 tablespoons Honey Dijon Vinaigrette (recipe opposite)

2 avocados, sliced

½ cup roasted and salted almonds, roughly chopped

½ cup golden raisins

Sesame seeds, for garnish

Flaky sea salt, for garnish

4 lemon wedges, for garnish

By now, it's pretty obvious that I love a bowl, and really want to convince you how great, easy, versatile, and delicious they are. This bowl is inspired by my standing order at my neighborhood superhero restaurant Superba. It's the coolest place! It's a bakery, restaurant, and community space that has the warmest vibe, great values, and has become my weekly healthy lunch spot in Venice, California. This bowl is my jet fuel, meant to put me in an equally cool and relaxed headspace. I love making it as part of weekly meal prep, too, when I'm whipping up components for a few meals. In this case I'll make rice, hard-boil a bunch of eggs, and whisk together a quick Honey Dijon Vinaigrette that is packed with health benefits. With these things handy, lunch can materialize in moments. But you can easily scale this down to a solo lunch, or make the full batch, store the dressing separately, and slice and add the avocado before serving.

Prep the grain bowl components: Cook the brown rice according to the package directions.

Meanwhile, fill a large bowl with ice and water. Add the eggs to a medium saucepan and add cold water to cover the eggs by 1 inch. Set the pan over high heat and bring to a rolling boil. Once boiling, cover the pan, remove from the heat, and set a timer for 8 minutes. After 8 minutes, place the eggs in the ice water and let sit for 8 minutes. Peel and cut in half lengthwise to serve.

Assemble the bowls: In a small bowl, toss the greens, carrot, and radish with 2 tablespoons of the dressing.

Divide the rice among 4 medium bowls. Top one side of each rice bowl with 2 egg halves and a few avocado slices. Place the salad on the other side of the rice and sprinkle the salad with the almonds and raisins. Garnish the whole bowl with sesame seeds, salt, and a lemon wedge. Pass extra dressing on the side!

Little Gem Salad with Toasted Bread Crumbs and Creamy Calabrian Chile Dressing

SERVES 4 / TOTAL TIME: 30 MINUTES
SPECIAL EQUIPMENT: IMMERSION BLENDER

CALABRIAN CHILE DRESSING

¼ cup extra-virgin olive oil

1 large egg yolk

1 oil-packed anchovy fillet, preferably Cento brand

1 garlic clove, peeled

1 tablespoon lemon juice

2 teaspoons red wine vinegar

½ teaspoon crushed Calabrian chile peppers (I love Tutto Calabria, available online)

½ teaspoon Dijon mustard

¼ teaspoon Worcestershire sauce

¼ teaspoon kosher salt

¼ teaspoon freshly ground black pepper

3 tablespoons finely grated Parmesan cheese

TOASTED BREAD CRUMBS

3 tablespoons extra-virgin olive oil

1 cup panko bread crumbs

½ teaspoon Italian seasoning

¼ teaspoon kosher salt

¼ teaspoon freshly ground black pepper

SALAD

3 to 4 heads Little Gem lettuce (about 5 ounces), washed and leaves separated

Grated Parmesan cheese, for garnish

Jon & Vinny's is a popular, relaxed LA restaurant known for its modern American twist on traditional Italian favorites. Everything they do just *works*—especially their Little Gem Salad. I know, I know, it's a salad . . . but I promise it's probably the *least* boring salad I've ever tried. The dressing is kind of a spicy Caesar dressing, used to great effect here but you'll want to use any left over to slather on toast, chicken breasts, veggies, grilled fish, almost everything. Little Gem lettuce is a cross between butter lettuce (also called Bibb and closely related to Boston) and romaine lettuce, but if you can't find it you can go with the more commonly found romaine. As with all salads, it's all about the Grocery Run ingredients (page 11). Get the best stuff you can find. Panko bread crumbs are a ready-made shortcut instead of croutons for crunch, and my fave Calabrian chiles bring a dependable level of sweet heat to the party. And a party is exactly what this salad is! At the restaurant they massage the dressing into each Little Gem leaf by hand, but it works just as well to drizzle on the dressing and top with bread crumbs right before you're about to serve. It goes great as a side for my Quick Rigatoni Bolognese (page 68) and Cheesy Garlic Bread with Warm Marinara (page 58).

Make the Calabrian chile dressing: In the cup that comes with the immersion blender (or in a small bowl with a whisk), combine the olive oil, egg yolk, anchovies, garlic, lemon juice, vinegar, chiles, mustard, Worcestershire sauce, salt, and pepper and blend until smooth. Stir in the Parmesan cheese. Feel free to give it a taste and adjust if you'd like with more chiles like I do!

Toast the bread crumbs: Heat the olive oil in a medium skillet over medium heat. Add the panko, Italian seasoning, salt, and pepper and cook, stirring frequently, until golden brown, 1 to 2 minutes. Transfer to a small bowl and set aside.

To serve, massage the lettuce with the dressing and arrange on a large plate or platter. Sprinkle the toasted bread crumbs over the top. Garnish with some Parm and serve.

Mom's Smashed Burgers with Mac Sauce

SERVES 4 / TOTAL TIME: 15 MINUTES
SPECIAL EQUIPMENT: MEAT SMASHER

MAC SAUCE

½ cup mayonnaise

2 tablespoons ketchup

½ teaspoon yellow mustard

1 tablespoon sweet relish

BURGERS

16 ounces ground beef, 80% lean

Kosher salt

Freshly ground black pepper

8 slices American cheese

ASSEMBLY

4 hamburger buns

3 tablespoons unsalted butter, at room temperature

1 cup shredded lettuce

¼ yellow onion, finely chopped

12 dill pickle chip slices

NOTE

We build these with relish, onions, and pickles but don't expect to find a tomato. That's the Stanton Smashed. But you do you!

I remember cringing every time my sister and I would beg for a McDonald's cheeseburger and my mom would say, "I can make it better at home!" Fast-forward to today, and here I am with an entire chapter in my cookbook dedicated to what? Making it better at home! I guess we really *do* all turn into our parents! So, thanks, Mom, this recipe is dedicated to you. I can admit it now, you really *could* make it better at home. I like to think of this recipe as an elevated fast-food burger you can whip up faster than heading to the drive-thru and back. The 80/20 ground beef blend is the key—fat is your friend here, it helps deliver the crunchy, tasty burger bits that are smash burger heaven. And there's really no reason to get fancy with the cheese. This is what slices of American were meant for! Make them inside a skillet, or I love using my flat top griddle on my grill outside. They're divine either way. Pro tip: Wrap your smashing device with parchment paper so the burger doesn't stick after you smash it. I serve these burgers with the baked fries from my California Burrito Bowl recipe (page 146), but I'm absolutely not claiming they are better than McDonald's fries. I'm not insane!

Make the Mac sauce: In a small bowl, stir together the mayonnaise, ketchup, mustard, and relish. Set aside while you prepare the burgers.

Make the burgers: Divide the meat into 8 equal portions and roll into balls. Heat a large cast-iron skillet or pan over medium-high heat. Place 2 balls of beef in the pan and smash them down with a stiff metal spatula or a meat smasher covered in parchment paper (you can buy one of these online for cheap and it's so worth it!) until the meat is thin and flat. Season lightly with salt and pepper. Using a large spatula, flip the burgers when the bottom is dark brown and crisp, about 2 minutes. Season this side lightly with salt and pepper and immediately add a slice of cheese. Cook for another minute then transfer to a platter and cover with foil to keep warm. Continue until all the burgers are cooked.

Toast the buns and build the burgers: Heat a skillet over medium-high heat. Split the buns and spread the butter over both insides of all the buns, place butter-side down to the hot skillet, and toast until golden brown and crispy, 1 to 2 minutes. (You can also broil them instead.) Spread both sides of the buns with your Mac sauce, top with the cheeseburgers, lettuce, onion, and pickles, and close the buns. Grab plenty of napkins and enjoy!

Spicy Tuna Crispy Rice

SERVES 4 / MAKES 18 PIECES / TOTAL TIME: 40 MINUTES, PLUS 1 HOUR FREEZING TIME

SUSHI RICE

Avocado or neutral oil, or baking spray

2 cups short-grain sushi rice

1 teaspoon sugar

1 teaspoon kosher salt

3 tablespoons rice vinegar

SPICY TUNA

8 ounces sushi-grade ahi tuna (salmon works, too!)

2 tablespoons mayonnaise, preferably Kewpie

2 teaspoons sriracha

1 teaspoon toasted sesame oil

2 teaspoons reduced-sodium soy sauce

1 tablespoon chopped green onion

¼ teaspoon kosher salt

⅛ teaspoon freshly ground black pepper

Avocado oil

1 jalapeño, thinly sliced

Reduced-sodium soy sauce for dipping

When I see that a restaurant serves spicy tuna crispy rice, all the other dishes listed on the menu go fuzzy because nothing else matters until I get some of it in front of me. And while I don't share well at the table, I'm happy to share this recipe! This is a pull-out-all-the-stops restaurant dish that will blow everyone at home away. Plus, it's an adventurous way to get a group involved in the cooking and assembling while you kick back and eat the spoils (just kidding). A few important things to remember: This is where you need to splurge on buying the freshest, highest-quality tuna at the best fish market, or even get it from the sushi counter, because you are eating this raw—no fooling around. Next, the cooked rice must be cool, but not cold, and unlike the rice for Hibachi-Style Fried Rice with Ginger Sauce (page 126), it should not be made the day before, because it will dry out and won't stick together enough to crisp up. Also, don't be stingy with the oil—you want CRISPY rice. It's in the title, for heaven's sake! A Lavender Haze cocktail (page 216) looks gorge alongside and will taste dreamy, too.

Using avocado oil, lightly oil and line an 8-inch square baking pan with parchment.

Rinse the rice in a fine strainer with cold water until the water runs clear. Add the rice and 2 cups of cold water to a saucepan with a lid. Let it sit uncovered for 15 minutes. Bring to a boil over medium heat, reduce heat to low, cover, and simmer for 15 minutes. Remove from the heat and let the rice sit, covered, for an additional 10 to 15 minutes. In a small saucepan set over medium heat, add the sugar, salt, and vinegar, bring to a boil, and let simmer until the sugar has dissolved. Stir the vinegar mixture into the rice and let cool for 10 to 15 minutes. Transfer the rice to the

baking pan and place in the freezer for 1 hour. This will help the rice rectangles keep their shape and make them easier to handle for panfrying.

Remove the rice from the freezer and let sit for 5 minutes. Using an offset spatula remove the rice from the baking pan and cut the rice into 18 rectangles, 2 inches x 1¼ inches.

Make the spicy tuna: Finely chop the tuna and add to a medium bowl. Stir in the mayonnaise, sriracha, sesame oil, soy sauce, green onion, salt, and pepper. Refrigerate while you fry the rice.

Line a plate with paper towels. Set a large skillet over medium-high heat and add enough avocado oil to

generously coat the bottom of the pan. Working in batches (the pieces shouldn't touch), when the oil is almost sizzling, add the rice rectangles to the pan and cook until golden brown and crisp on both sides, 1 to 2 minutes per side. Transfer to the paper towels to

drain. Add more oil as needed for the remaining batches.

To serve, top each rice patty with about 1 tablespoon of the tuna mixture and a slice of jalapeño, alongside soy sauce for dipping.

California Burrito Bowl

CARNE ASADA

1½ pounds skirt or flank steak

½ cup finely chopped fresh cilantro

4 garlic cloves, finely chopped

½ jalapeño, finely chopped (seeded for less heat)

Juice of 1 orange

Juice of 2 limes

2 tablespoons avocado oil

1 tablespoon apple cider vinegar

1 tablespoon reduced-sodium soy sauce

1 teaspoon ground cumin

1 teaspoon kosher salt

½ teaspoon freshly ground black pepper

CRISPY OVEN FRIES

2 russet potatoes, peeled

1 tablespoon extra-virgin olive oil

1 teaspoon kosher salt

¼ teaspoon freshly ground black pepper

BURRITO BOWL

3 cups Perfect Stovetop Rice (page 84)

1 cup shredded Mexican blend cheese

Guacamole (recipe follows)

½ cup sour cream

Hot sauce, for serving

When I was going to school at San Diego State, I was introduced to the classic California burrito and my life was changed forever. If you're not familiar with this magnificent creation, it's a football-size burrito filled with carne asada, French fries, cheese, guacamole, and sour cream. There are few things in this world that taste better, especially at two a.m. after a night of carousing (or so I'm told . . .). My frat party days are over (thank god), but my favorite late-night craving hasn't gone anywhere, so I came up with this reasonably sized (not as big as a newborn baby anymore), make-at-home version that still packs all the flavor. The carne asada is made with lean flank steak, which cooks up nicely on the stovetop (or grill). Just remember to slice your steaks against the grain—cut across the lines in the meat—for the most tender slices of beef. This recipe also has a bonus—my ride-or-die guac. Make it once and you'll make it again (and again). I guarantee. College may (or may not) be a long time ago for you, but this classic will help you develop your own, all-new cravings.

Start the carne asada: Place the steak in a large zip-seal plastic bag or lidded container. Add the cilantro, garlic, jalapeño, orange juice, lime juice, avocado oil, vinegar, soy sauce, cumin, salt, and pepper and gently rub the marinade into the meat. Refrigerate for at least 2 hours, preferably overnight.

Make the crispy oven fries: Preheat the oven to 425°F. Line a sheet pan with parchment paper.

Fill a large bowl with ice and water. Peel the potatoes and cut in half across the middle, and then cut each half into thin slices lengthwise, then stack and cut into thin strips lengthwise, resembling shoestring fries. As you work, place the fries in the cold water and soak for 20 minutes.

Drain the potatoes and use paper towels or kitchen towels to dry the potatoes very well. Arrange on the lined sheet pan and toss them with the olive oil, salt, and pepper.

Bake for 20 minutes. Flip the potatoes over and continue baking until golden and crisp, about 15 minutes longer.

Cook the carne asada: Remove the steak from the refrigerator about 15 minutes before cooking.

Heat a cast-iron skillet over medium-high heat. Remove the steak from the marinade and place in the hot pan, sear on both sides, and cook to rare (125° to 130°F), about 5 minutes per side, or medium-rare (135° to 140°F), about 8 minutes per side, testing by inserting an instant-read thermometer at an angle into the center of the steak. Remove the steak and let it rest for 8 minutes before thinly slicing across the grain. (I like the steak extra crispy, so I return the slices to a hot skillet and cook until crispy, 3 to 5 minutes.)

Divide the rice between 4 large shallow bowls. Add the steak slices and fries and top with cheese, guacamole, and sour cream. Pass the hot sauce!

Guacamole

MAKES ABOUT 1¾ CUPS

3 avocados, halved and pitted

1 ripe Roma tomato, finely chopped

¼ cup finely chopped red onion

1 jalapeño, finely chopped (seeded for less heat)

2 tablespoons finely chopped fresh cilantro

Juice of 1 lime, plus more to taste

½ teaspoon salt

¼ teaspoon freshly ground black pepper

Scoop the avocado flesh into a medium bowl and mash with a fork. Add the tomato, onion, jalapeño, cilantro, lime juice, salt, and pepper and stir to evenly combine. Add more salt, pepper, or lime juice to taste. Cover the surface with plastic wrap and refrigerate until ready to serve.

NOTE

Instead of serving this in bowls, you can make individual burritos with burrito-size flour tortillas.

MAJOR MAINS

I went back and forth for a while on what to name this chapter. In someone else's cookbook these might be the big dishes for "entertaining," but that felt too limited for me. I don't really believe in rules when it comes to entertaining. Because otherwise it starts to feel like a chore, and that's the total opposite of what it's supposed to be! I think hosting guests should be based on your mood, event, season, and size, from big and formal to totally last minute. Big wow-factor dishes or an awesome meal made up of a little bit of a lot of things (see Apps, Always, page 35). So as a super-relaxed hostess with quite a few successful dinner parties under my belt, these recipes are my standouts. They stay true to the simplicity of my cooking but take on more decadence than the recipes in other chapters, whether by using a bit more butter and cheese or using a pricier protein, like scallops or steak. These recipes are leveled-up from the average weeknight meal and deliver major flavor. Something special for a group or sexy date night, or anytime you want to put a little extra into your solo dinner and celebrate yourself (self-care is critical). These knockout dishes are designed for any skill level, like the Carnitas Taco Bar (page 152)—where after a bit of searing, the rest of the work is basically just simmering—or an almost effortless Creamy Cajun Butter Shrimp (page 159). Dad's Oven-Baked Jammy Ribs (page 177) are enjoyable year-round because you "barbecue" them to perfection in the oven, and my Carbonara Risotto (page 169) is a delicious mash-up of two classics. And I wouldn't leave you without two killer steak recipes, including a no-fail Balsamic Skirt Steak with Chimichurri and Blistered Tomatoes (page 160). These mains *are* major. I promise.

Carnitas Taco Bar

SERVES 6 / TOTAL TIME: 2½ HOURS

Taco bars, where you can make up your plate exactly as you like it, are always a hit, so this recipe is on fast repeat. It's a crowd-pleaser and a big kitchen confidence booster because you can't really mess it up—it's basically no-fail. And not to toot my own horn, but multiple people have declared these are the best carnitas they've ever had, and I agree (toot, toot). The pork is simmered uncovered, which helps it absorb all the saucy goodness, so you end up with perfectly tender meat that pretty much shreds itself, and a quick stir in a hot pan for addictive crispy bits. All you have to provide are the sides (which you can make or totally buy) and the tunes. These carnitas are great in tacos, added to a rice bowl, or even on top of my Elote Nachos (page 38). You'll have plenty of time to make a batch of Blackberry Mexican Mules (page 231) while they simmer! (If your friends are guac fiends, you might want to double the recipe.)

PORK CARNITAS

2½ to 3 pounds boneless pork shoulder or butt

2 teaspoons chili powder

2 teaspoons ground cumin

2 teaspoons kosher salt

1 teaspoon dried oregano

1 teaspoon sweet paprika

1 teaspoon freshly ground black pepper

½ teaspoon red chile flakes

¼ teaspoon ground cinnamon

2 tablespoons avocado oil

1 yellow onion, roughly chopped

5 garlic cloves, peeled but whole

Juice of 2 oranges

Juice of 2 limes

TACO BAR

2½ dozen small corn tortillas (or 1 dozen large almond or flour tortillas)

Guacamole (page 147) (about 1¾ cups)

2 cups sour cream

2 red onions, chopped

½ cup chopped fresh cilantro

3 limes, quartered

NOTE

To make in a slow cooker, season the pork and sauté as directed. Add to a slow cooker with the other ingredients but omit the water. Cover and cook on high for 7 hours or on low for 10 hours.

Make the pork carnitas: Cut the pork into 2-inch chunks, cutting off any large pieces of fat. In a large bowl, combine the pork, chili powder, cumin, salt, oregano, paprika, pepper, chile flakes, and cinnamon. Toss until the pork is coated.

Heat the avocado oil in a large Dutch oven over medium heat. Working in batches, add the pork and cook until a nice crust forms, about 1 minute per side. Return all of the meat to the pan and add enough water to cover the pork, about 5 cups. Add the onion, garlic, orange juice, and lime juice. Bring to a boil, then reduce the heat to low and simmer, uncovered, until the pork is very soft and tender, 1½ to 2 hours. (You can also do this in a slow cooker; see Note.)

Once the pork is soft and easily broken up with tongs, increase the heat to medium. Continue to cook, stirring the pork with the tongs until the liquid is fully absorbed and the pork is falling apart and can be easily shredded. For crispy carnitas, increase the heat to medium-high and cook, stirring occasionally, until the pork is browned and crisp, 5 to 7 minutes. Alternatively, spread the shredded carnitas on a foil-lined sheet pan and broil for 2 to 3 minutes until crisp.

Set up the taco bar: Wrap the tortillas in a damp paper towel and microwave for 30 seconds to 1 minute until warm. Set out the tortillas, carnitas, guacamole, sour cream, red onions, cilantro, and lime wedges.

Brown Butter–Lemon Halibut with Asparagus and Olive Oil Whipped Potatoes

SERVES 4 / TOTAL TIME: 45 MINUTES

- 1½ pounds halibut, skin removed, cut into 4 portions
- ¾ teaspoon kosher salt
- Freshly ground black pepper
- 2 tablespoons extra-virgin olive oil
- 1 pound asparagus, ends trimmed
- ⅓ cup unsalted butter
- 3 garlic cloves, finely chopped
- Juice of 1 lemon, plus wedges for squeezing
- Chopped fresh parsley, for garnish
- Olive Oil Whipped Potatoes (page 154)

I always used to go for a beautiful piece of fish accompanied by velvety mashed potatoes when I would go to a nice restaurant, until I realized it's often the priciest dish on the menu and I could make my own easy version at home for a fraction of the cost. One of my goals with this book is to show you that sometimes the most delicious things you can eat are some of the simplest, and this recipe proves it. If halibut is a bit steep for your budget, this dish is just as good with something a little easier on the wallet like tilapia or salmon steaks. For the whipped potatoes, using extra-virgin olive oil instead of butter adds a peppery fragrance and changes the usual homey mashed into fancier restaurant fare. Pair with my Texas Sheet Cake with Olive Oil Chocolate Frosting (page 248) to show your guests just how versatile the amazing olive is.

Season both sides of the halibut with ½ teaspoon kosher salt and a few twists of pepper and set aside. Heat the olive oil in a large skillet over medium-high heat. Add the halibut and cook until the flesh is opaque in the center, 3 to 4 minutes per side. Remove the fish to a serving platter and cover lightly with foil. Add the asparagus to the pan and season with remaining salt and pepper. Cook, stirring frequently, until browned and slightly softened, 3 to 4 minutes. Place the asparagus next to the fish on the serving platter.

Lower the heat to medium and add the butter and garlic to the skillet and cook until the butter is foamy and lightly browned, 1 to 2 minutes. Stir in the lemon juice and remove from the heat and spoon the sauce over the fish. Garnish with parsley and serve with lemon wedges for squeezing.

Serve with a bowl of the Olive Oil Whipped Potatoes.

Olive Oil Whipped Potatoes

SERVES 4

2 teaspoons kosher salt for boiling the potatoes

1¼ pounds Yukon Gold potatoes, peeled and cut into 1-inch dice

3 garlic cloves, peeled but whole

3 tablespoons extra-virgin olive oil

Kosher salt

Freshly ground black pepper

In a large pot of boiling salted water, cook the potatoes and garlic until the potatoes are tender when pierced with a fork, 10 to 15 minutes. Reserving 1 cup of the cooking water, drain thoroughly and return to the pot.

Using a potato masher or handheld mixer, mash the potatoes and garlic with 2 tablespoons of the olive oil. Add a few tablespoons of water at a time until the potatoes are smooth and creamy. Season with salt and pepper to taste.

Just before serving, drizzle with the remaining 1 tablespoon of olive oil.

Perfect Cast-Iron Steaks and Crispy Cacio e Pepe Potatoes

SERVES 4 / TOTAL TIME: 45 MINUTES

2 boneless steaks, such as rib eye or New York strip, 1 inch thick (8 to 10 ounces each)

½ teaspoon kosher salt

¼ teaspoon freshly ground black pepper

2 tablespoons extra-virgin olive oil

2 tablespoons salted butter

2 garlic cloves, smashed and peeled

1 shallot, peeled and halved lengthwise

4 fresh thyme sprigs

3 fresh rosemary sprigs

Freshly ground black pepper

Lemon wedges, for serving

Crispy Cacio e Pepe Potatoes (recipe follows)

NOTE

Throw some zucchini or asparagus in the skillet right after you remove the steak. It will cook quickly and have tons of flavor. A great way to have a delicious vegetable side without much effort.

I turned to my girlfriend group for help, asking them "What would you cook for your significant other if you were celebrating something special?" For the first time in our group text history, fifteen girls unanimously agreed on something. A nice, juicy steak. I am not here to help you figure out why so many people insist that steak is the best date night meal there is, but I will provide you with the tools you need to make the most perfect cast-iron steak your partner will ever have. All you need is a great steak, a scorchingly hot skillet, some garlic, shallots, and herbs, and happiness is yours.

This is also a good time to up your potato game with these Crispy Cacio e Pepe Potatoes, an ode to one of my favorite cheesy, peppery pasta dishes, with the added bonus of crispy potato skins. Shake up a batch of my Dirty Martinis (page 223) and you've mastered date night.

Gently pat the steaks dry with paper towels. Season both sides with the salt and pepper. Set aside to bring to room temperature, about 30 minutes. This is crucial to ensure your steak cooks perfectly!

Heat a cast-iron skillet over medium-high heat for about 5 minutes. Add the oil and once the oil starts smoking, add the steaks and cook, until browned on both sides, about 3 minutes per side.

Reduce the heat to medium-low. Add the butter, garlic, shallot, thyme, and rosemary. Carefully tilt the pan to create a pool of foamy, melted butter. Spoon the butter over the top of the steaks, repeating until the internal temperature reaches 125°F for rare, 135°F for medium-rare, or until your desired degree of doneness.

Transfer the steaks to a cutting board to rest for 5 minutes before slicing against the grain.

Plate the sliced steak and spoon the pan juices over them. Top with a few twists of pepper and a squeeze of lemon. Serve with the Crispy Cacio e Pepe Potatoes.

Crispy Cacio e Pepe Potatoes

SERVES 4

2 russet potatoes, peeled and cut into 1- to 1½-inch cubes

1 teaspoon kosher salt

2 tablespoons extra-virgin olive oil

3 tablespoons grated Parmesan cheese

1 teaspoon freshly ground black pepper

Preheat the oven to 425°F. Line a large sheet pan with foil.

Place the potatoes in a large pot and add cold water to cover by 2 inches. Add ½ teaspoon salt and bring to a boil. Cook until the potatoes are slightly tender when pierced with a fork, about 10 minutes.

Drain thoroughly and transfer the potatoes to a large bowl. Add the olive oil, Parmesan, pepper, and remaining ½ teaspoon of salt. Toss to coat. Don't be afraid to get rough! By breaking up the outside of the potatoes a bit, you will ensure that they get nice and crispy.

Arrange the potatoes on the prepared sheet pan in an even layer and roast until golden on the bottom, about 20 minutes. Flip the potatoes, return to the oven, and roast until golden brown and crispy, 8 to 10 minutes. Serve hot.

Creamy Cajun Butter Shrimp

SERVES 4 / TOTAL TIME: 30 MINUTES

1½ pounds shrimp, peeled and deveined, tails left on

¾ teaspoon kosher salt

½ teaspoon freshly ground black pepper

2 tablespoons extra-virgin olive oil

1½ sticks (6 ounces) unsalted butter

½ yellow onion, finely chopped

4 garlic cloves, finely chopped

1 tablespoon Cajun seasoning

2 teaspoons chopped fresh rosemary

1 cup chicken broth

½ cup heavy cream

Juice of ½ lemon, plus more to taste

Crusty bread, Perfect Stovetop Rice (page 84), or pasta (see Note), for serving

The inspiration for this recipe comes from my parents and me riffing in their kitchen, playing around with shrimp ideas and taking turns at bat at the stove . . . the resulting dish was so good, we fought over the last shrimp (I won). The sauce is rich and decadent from the butter and cream, while also perfectly flavored from the fresh herbs and the spices in the Cajun seasoning. You may seriously consider bathing in it. I'm really proud of how it came out. Funny story: When I was recipe testing for this book, I posted a picture of this dish on my IG story and my DMs blew up with people asking for the recipe. So here you have it, one year later. Sorry for the wait, but it's worth it!

Pat the shrimp dry with a paper towel and lay flat on a large plate or sheet pan. Season both sides evenly with the salt and pepper.

Heat the olive oil in a large skillet over medium-high heat. Add the shrimp in an even layer and cook until slightly golden, about 1 minute per side. The shrimp will not be completely cooked, as they will finish cooking in the sauce. Remove and set aside.

In the same skillet, melt the butter. Reduce the heat to medium, add the onion and garlic, and cook, stirring occasionally, until the onion is translucent, about 4 minutes.

Add the Cajun seasoning and rosemary and stir until fragrant, about 30 seconds. Add the chicken broth, cream, and lemon juice, stir, and bring to a boil. Reduce the heat and simmer until the sauce has reduced by half, 3 to 4 minutes.

Return the shrimp to the pan, stir to coat with the sauce, and simmer until the shrimp are opaque throughout, about 1½ minutes. Taste and add more salt, pepper, and/or lemon juice if needed.

Serve with crusty bread, Perfect Stovetop Rice (page 84), or even your favorite pasta to soak up the sauce.

NOTE

The easiest solution for keeping this meal quick is to serve the shrimp with sliced bread (no cooking involved). But if you choose rice or pasta and want to keep this meal at its speedy 30 minutes, you just need to start cooking them right after you sear the shrimp at the very beginning.

Balsamic Skirt Steak
with Chimichurri and Blistered Tomatoes

SERVES 4 / TOTAL TIME: 1 HOUR

CHIMICHURRI SAUCE

1 cup finely chopped fresh cilantro

½ cup finely chopped fresh parsley

⅓ cup extra-virgin olive oil

2 tablespoons red wine vinegar

2 garlic cloves, finely chopped

⅓ jalapeño, finely chopped (seeded for less heat)

¼ teaspoon kosher salt

BALSAMIC SKIRT STEAK

⅓ cup balsamic vinegar

2 tablespoons extra-virgin olive oil

2 garlic cloves, finely chopped

1 teaspoon kosher salt

½ teaspoon freshly ground black pepper

1½ pounds skirt steak

1 tablespoon extra-virgin olive oil

16 ounces cherry tomatoes

NOTE

Unless you really prefer your meat very rare, I let my meat rest, and after the tomatoes have blistered, I get my pan very hot, add a tiny bit of olive oil, and add the meat back for about a minute so it's extra crispy.

If there's one perfect combination in the world of food, it's a beautifully seared steak topped with chimichurri, the Argentinian salsa that's a ton of parsley and garlic mixed with oil and vinegar. It's another example of a homemade sauce taking your dish to another level! Plus, it not only *can*, but *should*, be made ahead of time (along with the steak marinade) so that the flavors really get to know each other and there's less work to do last minute— a win-win! Skirt steak feels like the perfect cut for this because it cooks really quickly and it's pretty hard to mess up. My move is to cook it a bit rarer than I like, then throw it back into the hot pan closer to serving time so all of the slices get a chance to crisp up and caramelize. Would not say no to seeing the Olive Oil Whipped Potatoes (page 154) alongside this dish, or even going casual with some tortillas to catch all that sauce.

Make the chimichurri sauce: In a medium bowl, combine the cilantro, parsley, olive oil, red wine vinegar, garlic, jalapeño, and salt. Cover and refrigerate until ready to serve. This can be made a day or so ahead of time if kept refrigerated.

Marinate and cook the skirt steak: In a zip-seal plastic bag or airtight container, combine the balsamic vinegar, olive oil, garlic, kosher salt, and pepper. Add the steak and turn to fully coat. Marinate for 30 minutes at room temperature (or refrigerate a day ahead).

Heat a grill pan or cast-iron skillet over medium-high heat. Add the marinated steak (letting any excess marinade drip off) and cook until the meat is well browned on both sides and an instant-read thermometer inserted in the center of the steak reads 135°F for medium-rare, 4 to 5 minutes per side. Transfer to a cutting board and let rest about 7 minutes so the steak retains its juices.

In the same pan, heat 1 tablespoon of the olive oil over medium heat. Add the tomatoes and season with a pinch of salt and a few twists of pepper. Cook until blistered, 2 to 3 minutes.

Slice the steak against the grain. Serve with the blistered tomatoes and top with the chimichurri sauce.

Mediterranean Roasted Chicken with Homemade (or Not) Flatbread

SERVES 4 TO 6 / TOTAL TIME: 1½ HOURS

ROASTED CHICKEN

3 tablespoons unsalted butter, at room temperature

2 tablespoons extra-virgin olive oil

4 garlic cloves, finely chopped

3 tablespoons finely chopped fresh oregano or 1½ tablespoons dried oregano

2 tablespoons finely chopped fresh dill or 1 tablespoon dried dill

2 teaspoons kosher salt

1 teaspoon freshly ground black pepper

Grated zest and juice of 1 lemon

1 whole chicken (4 to 5 pounds), giblets removed

FOR SERVING

6 (6- to 8-inch) Homemade Flatbread (recipe follows), or store-bought

3 cucumbers, thinly sliced

3 ripe beefsteak tomatoes, sliced

1 red onion, thinly sliced

Jalapeño Tzatziki (page 115)

White Bean Hummus (page 62)

Feta cheese, crumbled

Chopped fresh herbs, such as mint or dill

Wraps with dips and sauces are kind of my thing. My other thing is not making dinner too fussy, and the beauty of this recipe is that you can choose just how much prep and cooking you want to do. I've made this chicken last minute and served it with store-bought dips and breads more times than I've made the whole meal from scratch. And that's okay—it's the whole point of the book—do what you can and what you want! While the freshly baked flatbread is totally worth the effort, if I had to make a choice between which one I would spend time on, the chicken is really the star of the show. It's one dish every home cook should master. I always spatchcock a whole chicken (I love that word!). I know it sounds intimidating, but it's really just a fancy way to say you're removing the backbone so it can lie flat and cook evenly (more quickly, too). You can ask your butcher to do it for you or follow the instructions here, which I learned from my dad. And one last push for trying to make the bread yourself—I'm really not the best baker, so I tried to make this as simple as possible. There's no yeast (yeast and I don't have a great track record! ha-ha)—so give it a shot. I promise you can do it.

Preheat the oven to 425°F.

Allow the Jalapeño Tzatziki and White Bean Hummus to come to room temperature if refrigerated.

Roast the chicken: In a small bowl, combine the butter, olive oil, garlic, oregano, dill, salt, pepper, and lemon zest (reserve the juice), and set aside.

Place the chicken on a cutting board breast-side down. With kitchen scissors or poultry shears, carefully cut along both sides of the backbone and remove. Flip the chicken over so the breast side is up. Press down firmly in the center of the breast with the heels of your hands until you hear a pop and the chicken lies flat. Transfer to a sheet pan or a large roasting pan.

Rub the butter-herb mixture generously on both sides of the chicken, and under the legs and wings. Drizzle both sides of the chicken with the lemon juice. Transfer to the oven and bake until the chicken thigh registers 165°F and the juices run clear, 45 to 50 minutes. (I like to broil for the last 2 to 3 minutes to crisp the skin.)

When the chicken is done, let it rest for at least 10 minutes before carving.

Carve your bird: Lay the chicken breast-side up on the cutting board. One with grooves is important so it catches the juices. If you don't have one, place a sheet pan under the cutting board to catch the juices. Gently pull the leg away from the body and, using a sharp knife, cut through the skin between the thigh leg and the body and cut through the joint. Repeat with the other leg.

Place the leg skin-side down and cut through the joint to separate the leg from the thigh. Repeat with the other leg. I keep the legs to snack on another time.

Then, slice the breast crosswise and set on a platter.

Next, using the breastbone as a guide, carve against the bone and remove the breast off the bone, keeping with the wing attached. Cut the wing at the joint and, again, save for snacking!

Slice the thigh meat off the bone and slice the meat crosswise and set on a platter.

To serve, set out a communal platter with the flatbread, veggies, dips, feta, and herbs for making wraps.

Homemade Flatbread

2 cups all-purpose flour, plus more for dusting

1 teaspoon baking soda

½ teaspoon sugar

¼ teaspoon kosher salt

2 tablespoons unsalted butter, at room temperature

1 cup warm water

3 tablespoons unsalted butter

In a large bowl, stir together the flour, baking soda, sugar, and salt until combined. Using your hands, add 2 tablespoons of the butter and combine well until the butter is fully incorporated into the flour mixture.

Add the warm water and combine until a dough forms and all the dry bits of flour are incorporated. If the dough is too sticky, add more flour. Be careful not to overmix! Cover with a kitchen towel and let sit at room temperature for 30 minutes.

After the dough has rested, knead it on a flour-dusted work surface until a smooth ball forms. Cut the dough into 6 equal portions and shape each into a ball. Using your hands, gently stretch each dough ball into an 8-inch round about ¼ inch thick. Remember, these don't need to be perfect circles or an even thickness throughout.

Heat a skillet over medium heat and add 1 tablespoon of the butter. Once melted add 1 flatbread and cook until golden brown, about 1 minute per side. Repeat with the remaining flatbread, adding butter to grease the pan as needed.

Pepperoni Cast-Iron Pan Pizza

SERVES 2 / TOTAL TIME: 30 MINUTES

½ pound store-bought pizza dough

3 tablespoons extra-virgin olive oil, plus more for drizzling

½ cup pizza sauce

3 ounces fresh mozzarella cheese, torn or shredded

2 ounces sliced pepperoni

¼ cup fresh basil leaves

Rosemary Hot Honey (from Panfried Brie, page 37), or 2 tablespoons honey and ¼ teaspoon red chile flakes, for garnish

While I'm not against pizza ovens, they just aren't all that practical or available to most of us. That said, I can get pretty close to a pizza-oven crust with this foolproof version made in a cast-iron pan. It's a pretty dramatic presentation, too, which I love. The cast-iron creates a sturdy crust that fulfills my dreams of a pizza that can withstand tons of delicious toppings without falling apart. And you can totally use this method on a grill, too! This is my favorite dinner to make when I have friends over before a night out. The pizzas are made in a 10-inch cast-iron skillet (also handy for Strawberry Skillet Galette [page 239]). I suggest you buy two if you host frequently so you can make multiples at a time for a crowd. This way everyone can hang out in the kitchen or back-yard, getting involved, personalizing their pies while we socialize. And, there's minimal mess, which kind of makes everything taste a little bit better, don't you think? To make this even more super quick and easy, I use good-quality store-bought dough that tastes—and behaves—like homemade. And as far as toppings, go crazy! These suggestions are merely a starting point. If you can dream it, you can (and probably should) put it on a pizza!

NOTE

If you haven't seasoned your cast-iron in a while, I suggest doing so before trying this recipe. You don't want the dough sticking to the pan!

Let the dough sit at room temperature for 30 minutes.

Position one rack in the lowest position and another in the top third of the oven and preheat the oven to 500°F.

Add 2 tablespoons of the olive oil to a 10-inch cast-iron skillet. Add the dough and toss to coat in the oil. Spread the dough out evenly to the edges of the pan. Spread the pizza sauce evenly all the way to the edges of the dough. Evenly top with the mozzarella, pepperoni, and basil.

Bake on the bottom rack until the cheese is melted and the crust is golden brown, 12 to 14 minutes. Move the pan and broil until the top is nice and bubbling, 1 to 2 minutes. Check the bottom of the pizza—if it's not super crispy, transfer the pan to the stovetop over medium-high heat and cook until browned and crispy, about 1 minute. Let cool for about 2 minutes in the pan and then transfer to a wire rack.

Drizzle with olive oil and hot honey and serve.

Buttery Seared Scallops

SERVES 4 / TOTAL TIME: 15 MINUTES

1 pound sea scallops (about 12 very large), side muscle removed

1 teaspoon kosher salt

2 tablespoons extra-virgin olive oil

2 tablespoons unsalted butter

Chopped fresh parsley, for garnish

1 lemon, ½ juiced and ½ cut into wedges for squeezing

Is there anything more beautiful or enticing than an expertly seared scallop? I'd be hard-pressed to think of anything more luxurious, and that's why I knew I had to include a recipe for them in this book—fat, juicy scallops with their golden-brown-crusted exterior and plump, moist centers. Problem was, until now they had been a restaurant-only fish for me. I had no clue how to cook them. After some research and trial and error, I came up with a technique that gets me the scallops of my dreams. For this recipe we're using the large, plump sea scallops, not the smaller, slightly sweeter bay scallops, which are better for soups. These will seriously impress at a dinner party or a fancy celebration dinner for a loved one. And don't be intimidated by the cooking part. This turned out to be one of the easiest things I've ever made, as I figured out it's all about drying them fully before they hit the pan and cooking them over medium-high heat to get that perfect sear. They're pretty wondrous served with my Carbonara Risotto (page 169).

NOTE

The inside of the scallops should be opaque and they should be firm, but buttery. If they are tough to cut, they are undercooked.

Pat the scallops dry with paper towels. Season both sides with the salt.

Heat the olive oil in a large skillet over medium-high heat. Add the scallops, making sure not to crowd, and cook for 3 minutes without moving. Flip, reduce the heat to medium, and add the butter. Once melted, tilt the pan slightly and baste the scallops with the melted butter until the scallops are cooked through (see Note), about 2 minutes.

Garnish the scallops with parsley and serve lemon wedges on the side for squeezing.

Carbonara Risotto

SERVES 4 / TOTAL TIME: 35 MINUTES

5½ cups chicken broth (or 4 cups broth plus 1½ cups water)

4 ounces diced pancetta

1½ cups Arborio rice

½ cup dry white wine, like Sauvignon Blanc

4 large egg yolks

¼ cup grated Parmesan cheese, plus more for serving

1 teaspoon freshly ground pepper, plus more for garnish

½ teaspoon kosher salt

I knew I wanted to include a risotto dish in this section because even though I make it all the time (despite what you may have heard, it's actually surprisingly easy to do), it still feels special every time that I eat it. I'm not sure how I dreamed up this carbonara/risotto mash-up, but I am so happy I did, because this dish has become one of my favorites, a decadent masterpiece.

Arborio rice is what you need to use here. It's an Italian short-grain rice with a high starch content, which when stirred regularly while slowly adding liquid in increments releases its starches to create that signature creamy sauce. The trick is to cook it so the sauce is creamy but the rice retains a slightly firm, chewy bite—the mark of an ideal risotto. I have to admit, this carbonara risotto really could be served at a restaurant, but I like it best on a cozy date night in, with a Tequila Negroni (page 215) and if you want to go all out add the Strawberry Skillet Galette (page 239). *Buon appetito!*

Fill a serving bowl with boiling water and cover with plastic wrap or foil to keep it warm for serving. (Alternatively, microwave the empty bowl for 30 to 45 seconds right before serving.)

In a medium saucepan, heat the chicken broth over medium-low heat and keep it warm.

Line a plate with paper towels.

In a cold large Dutch oven or large pot, add the pancetta and set the pan over medium heat. Cook the pancetta, stirring occasionally, until crisp, about 7 minutes. Using a slotted metal spoon, scoop the pancetta onto the paper towels to drain. Remove all but 2 tablespoons of the fat in the pan and discard.

Set the pan over medium-low heat. Using a wooden spoon, stir in the rice to coat with the fat and toast the rice, stirring occasionally, for 1 minute. Add the wine and stir until it is absorbed by the rice. Add 1 cup of the warm chicken broth and stir until it is almost absorbed by the rice. If you can drag the spoon through the middle of the pot and see the bottom without any liquid you will know it's time to add more liquid. Continue to add the broth in small amounts and cook, stirring constantly until the sauce is creamy and the rice is firm to the bite (like an al dente pasta), about 30 minutes. Remove from the heat and cover to keep hot.

In a small bowl, whisk together the egg yolks, Parmesan, pepper, and salt. Whisk this into the hot rice until evenly distributed and stir in the reserved pancetta.

Remove the hot water, dry the serving bowl, and transfer the risotto to the bowl. Top with more Parmesan and garnish with a few twists of pepper.

NOTE

The recipe uses more than 4 cups of broth, and if you're like me and don't want to open another container of chicken broth, I promise you can substitute water for the last 1½ cup of broth.

Meme's Chicken Tagine

SERVES 4 / TOTAL TIME: 30 MINUTES

SPICE MIX

Grated zest of 1 lemon

1 tablespoon sweet paprika

2 teaspoons ground cumin

1½ teaspoons kosher salt

1 teaspoon ground coriander

1 teaspoon ground turmeric

½ teaspoon ground cinnamon

½ teaspoon ground ginger

½ teaspoon freshly ground
black pepper

¼ teaspoon red chile flakes

CHICKEN TAGINE

1½ pounds boneless, skinless
chicken thighs

2 tablespoons extra-virgin
olive oil

1 white onion, thinly sliced

5 garlic cloves, finely
chopped

1 medium eggplant, cut into
1-inch dice

4 large carrots, peeled and
cut into 1-inch dice

1 (15-ounce) can chickpeas,
drained and rinsed

½ cup pitted green olives,
such as Castelvetrano (or
your favorite)

1 tablespoon chopped fresh
parsley

½ cup chicken broth

Juice of 1 lemon

FOR SERVING

4 cups cooked couscous

3 tablespoons finely chopped
fresh parsley, for garnish

1½ tablespoons finely
chopped fresh mint, for
garnish

A personal and blog favorite, this is my spin on a traditional Moroccan tagine that I learned when I was little when I would help my Moroccan grandmother, Meme, in the kitchen. If you've never had tagine, it's one of the world's best dishes (though I'm clearly biased). It's a fragrant, flavorful stew with vegetables and a protein—like chicken, lamb, beef, or even fish—all perfumed by the spices of North Africa and served with couscous. It gets the name tagine from the pot it's traditionally cooked in—a beautiful clay pot with a cone-shaped lid, but you can use a Dutch oven or heavy-bottomed pot with a lid. Feel free to add your favorite veggie or swap the chicken for a different protein.

Make the spice mix: In a small bowl, combine the lemon zest, paprika, cumin, salt, coriander, turmeric, cinnamon, ginger, pepper, and chile flakes. Measure out 2 tablespoons of the spice mix and set aside for the vegetables.

Make the tagine: In a medium bowl, coat the chicken thighs with the remaining spice mix and massage the spice mix into the chicken until fully coated.

Heat the oil in a large Dutch oven, the base of a flameproof tagine, or a large skillet with a lid over medium heat. Add the chicken and cook until lightly browned, about 2 minutes per side (not cooked through; it will cook more with the vegetables). Transfer the chicken to a plate and set aside.

Add the onion and garlic to the pan and cook, stirring, until softened, about 7 minutes. Add the eggplant and carrots, season with the reserved spice mix, and cook, stirring occasionally, until the vegetables are softened, 5 to 6 minutes.

Add the chickpeas, olives, and parsley and stir to combine. Set the chicken thighs back on top. Pour the chicken broth and half the lemon juice over everything. Reduce the heat to low, cover, and simmer until the vegetables and chicken are fully cooked and the sauce has thickened, about 15 minutes.

Stir in the remaining lemon juice just before serving. Serve the tagine over couscous and garnish with the parsley and mint.

Pesto Meatballs with Whipped Ricotta

SERVES 4 / TOTAL TIME: 40 MINUTES

1 pound ground beef, 85% lean

⅓ cup almond flour (for gluten-free meatballs) or plain bread crumbs

¼ cup Basil Pesto (page 73), plus more for serving

1 large egg

¾ teaspoon kosher salt

½ teaspoon freshly ground black pepper

16 ounces whole-milk ricotta cheese

2 tablespoons extra-virgin olive oil

Crusty bread, for serving

This recipe is kind of comically easy to make, but don't tell your guests that. It can be our little secret. One thing I will ask is that, since it's so simple, let's agree to use the best ingredients you can find. It always makes a difference. So that means making your own homemade pesto. It's really easy and trust me, you will never go back. Whip it up the day before if that works best for you, it will taste even better. Then the meatball mixture is equally breezy to throw together. Great extra-virgin olive oil and light and fluffy fresh ricotta are the A-listers you need to use to make this dish sing. Round this main course out with Shaved Brussels Sprouts Salad with Parmesan and Grapes (page 101) and an Aperol Slushie (page 220), or I wouldn't say no to this served mini-meatball-size as an app, either. BRB, going to the store to make this right now.

Preheat the oven to 400°F. Line a sheet pan with parchment paper.

Make the meatballs: In a large bowl, using your hands or a wooden spoon, gently combine the beef, flour (or bread crumbs), pesto, egg, ½ teaspoon of the salt, and pepper. Using a tablespoon, form into about 20 meatballs the size of golf balls.

Arrange on the sheet pan and bake until browned and cooked through, about 16 minutes, turning the meatballs midway through baking.

Whip the ricotta: While the meatballs are baking, in a food processor, combine the ricotta, olive oil, and remaining ¼ teaspoon of the salt and blend on high until the ricotta is light and fluffy, 30 seconds to 1 minute. Lightly cover and refrigerate until ready to serve.

Spread the whipped ricotta on a platter or individual plates topped with the meatballs. Drizzle with more pesto. Serve with crusty bread for dipping. YUM!!!

Dad's Oven-Baked Jammy Ribs

SERVES 4 TO 6 / TOTAL TIME: 3½ HOURS

RIB PACKETS

2 (2½-pound) racks baby back ribs (about 5 pounds total)

¼ cup packed light brown sugar

3 tablespoons kosher salt

2 tablespoons garlic powder

2 tablespoons smoked paprika

1 tablespoon onion powder

2 teaspoons mustard powder

1 teaspoon red chile flakes

1 cup light lager beer, like Pacifico, optional

JAMMY BBQ SAUCE

1 cup seedless raspberry or peach jam

1 (4½-ounce) tube double concentrate tomato paste or 6-ounce can tomato paste

½ cup ketchup

2 tablespoons hot sauce (preferably Cholula)

2 tablespoons Worcestershire sauce

1 tablespoon apple cider vinegar

1 tablespoon reduced-sodium soy sauce

1 tablespoon yellow mustard

½ teaspoon kosher salt

½ teaspoon freshly ground black pepper

One of my favorite foods in the world is ribs. If they're on the menu at a restaurant, I'll order them—even if I'm on a first date (yes, I've done it). I think it's because I grew up eating the best ribs in the world, made by my awesome dad, mastered over his many years of experience cooking ribs for our family. He slow-smokes his for hours in an outdoor smoker, but my mission was to make exceptional ribs like he does, but in the oven. So I dragged him in the kitchen to experiment in the oven, and we were both seriously impressed by the outcome. Most of the work with my version is done during the last half hour when you baste and baste, leading up to a broil to build up that classic backyard-smoker-style crust. You can even do most of this recipe a day ahead and rewarm the ribs wrapped in foil and finish with the last baste and broil. I also love to finish these off on the grill for that irreplaceable char. My neighbor growing up always added a Mexican lager to his ribs, so we tested it that way. It definitely adds a nice flavor and makes the ribs more tender, but it isn't 100 percent necessary. I've used seedless raspberry jam in the sauce, but I'm sure your favorite flavor would work just as well!

Preheat the oven to 300°F. Line 2 sheet pans with foil.

Assemble the rib packets: Remove the membrane from the backside of the racks by holding a sharp paring knife horizontally and pushing the sharp tip of the knife between the rib and the membrane. Twist it so the dull side is up and pull up until the membrane lifts up enough for you to put your finger under it. Gently pull the membrane off.

In a medium bowl, add the brown sugar, salt, garlic powder, paprika, onion powder, mustard powder, and chile flakes. Stir to combine evenly.

Pull off 2 lengths of heavy-duty foil each large enough to enclose one of the racks in a leakproof package. Place a rack on each length of foil and rub both sides of the ribs with the dry rub. Pour ½ cup of beer into each packet on the bottom of the foil and carefully seal. Place both packets on the lined sheet pans.

Bake for 2 hours.

Using tongs and being careful of the steam, open up the foil packets and increase the oven temperature to 350°F. Bake for an additional 20 minutes.

Meanwhile, make the jammy BBQ sauce: In a small saucepan, combine the jam, tomato paste, ketchup, hot sauce, Worcestershire sauce, vinegar, soy sauce, mustard, ½ teaspoon of the salt, and ½ teaspoon of the black pepper. Bring to a simmer over medium heat and remove from the heat.

After the ribs have been in for 2 hours 20 minutes, remove them from the oven and brush the BBQ sauce on both sides of the ribs. Return to the oven and bake until the sauce is almost dried and tacky, 7 to 10 minutes.

Brush a second coat of sauce only on the top and sides and bake until the sauce is dried and tacky, about 7 minutes.

Brush a third coat of sauce on the top and sides and bake until the sauce is dried and tacky, about 7 minutes.

Switch the oven to broil (or finish on the grill). Brush a fourth coat of sauce on the top and broil (or grill) until the ribs are nice and crispy, 2 to 3 minutes.

Let cool for 5 minutes, slice between the ribs, and serve.

Twice-Baked Cheesy Spaghetti Squash

SERVES 4 / TOTAL TIME: 1 HOUR 15 MINUTES

1 medium spaghetti squash (about 2 pounds) (see Tip)

1 tablespoon extra-virgin olive oil

1 teaspoon kosher salt

½ teaspoon freshly ground black pepper

1 cup panko bread crumbs

3 tablespoons extra-virgin olive oil

2 tablespoons grated Parmesan cheese

2 garlic cloves, finely chopped

½ teaspoon Italian seasoning

¼ teaspoon kosher salt

¼ teaspoon freshly ground black pepper

2 tablespoons extra-virgin olive oil

2 tablespoons unsalted butter

2 cloves garlic, finely chopped

1 tablespoon all-purpose flour

1 cup whole milk, warmed

1 cup shredded mozzarella cheese

½ teaspoon kosher salt

½ teaspoon freshly ground black pepper

¼ teaspoon red chile flakes

Chopped fresh parsley, for garnish

I want to start by saying I am not a big fan of replacing carbs with vegetables, unless it's a gluten thing (whoever came up with cauliflower rice and zoodles has some bad karma coming their way lol!). However, spaghetti squash is another story. You can't compare it to spaghetti beyond the way it looks—I mean the flavors are totally different—but there's something to be said about the way the sweetness and creaminess of the squash is the ideal partner for a cheesy pasta sauce. I love serving spaghetti squash for friends because they're always shocked at how good it tastes, especially when I use this recipe. It kind of feels like a sweeter mac and cheese or an amazing holiday side dish—though I eat it year-round. For an even lighter version, just roast it along with some chicken thighs and peppers, tomatoes, and asparagus for a nice sheet pan spaghetti. Use your imagination and play around!

Bake the spaghetti squash: Preheat the oven to 400°F. Line a sheet pan with foil.

Carefully halve the squash lengthwise. Remove the seeds with a spoon. Spread the olive oil on the inside and outside of the squash and season the inside with the salt and pepper.

Place on the sheet pan cut-side down and bake until the squash is tender and the flesh can be easily scraped with a fork into "spaghetti," 35 to 45 minutes.

Meanwhile, make the garlic bread crumbs: In a small bowl, stir together the panko, olive oil, Parmesan, garlic, Italian seasoning, salt, and pepper until evenly combined. Set aside.

Make the cheese sauce: About 15 minutes before the squash is done, heat the olive oil and butter in a medium Dutch oven or pot over medium heat. Once the butter is melted, add the garlic and cook, stirring, until softened and fragrant, 1 to 2 minutes. Whisk in the flour and cook, stirring, until it is lightly toasted, about 45 seconds. Slowly whisk in the milk and cook, stirring constantly, until thickened, about 2 minutes. Stir in the mozzarella, salt, pepper, and chile flakes and continue to stir until the cheese has melted and the sauce has thickened. Remove from the heat and cover to keep warm.

When the squash is done baking, remove from the oven but leave the oven on. As soon as the squash is cool enough to handle (but still hot), use a fork to carefully scrape the flesh out of the skins into spaghetti-like strands into a large bowl. Take care not to damage the skin, as you will use them as "boats" for the next step.

Add the squash strands to the cheese sauce and toss to fully coat. Taste and add more salt and pepper, if needed. Fill the hollowed squash skins with the squash-and-cheese mixture and set back on the sheet pan. Top with the garlic bread crumbs.

Return to the oven and bake until the bread crumbs are golden brown, about 15 minutes.

To serve, cut each squash in half and garnish with parsley.

TIP

Pop the spaghetti squash in the microwave for a few minutes before cutting it in half to make it easier to cut!

One-Pot Creamy Shells with Peas and Bacon

SERVES 6 / TOTAL TIME: 20 MINUTES

6 slices bacon, roughly chopped

8 ounces frozen peas

2 garlic cloves, finely chopped

1 tablespoon all-purpose flour

1 teaspoon garlic powder

1 teaspoon sweet paprika

1 teaspoon kosher salt

1 teaspoon freshly ground black pepper

3 cups chicken broth

½ cup half-and-half

1 pound medium pasta shells

½ cup grated Parmesan cheese

1 tablespoon fresh thyme leaves, for garnish

When I'm making a dish for a dinner party, I usually lean toward something crowd-pleasing with minimal cleanup. This recipe came out of a very specific craving for a super-savory, creamy pasta. I knew I wanted there to be bacon and peas, because that's such an all-star combo, but I also wanted to make it one-pot friendly, because no one likes to do a ton of dishes. Here's the result. It's a little more decadent than something you might whip up for a Monday or Tuesday night, but it's one of my favorite things to make when I have friends over on the weekends because it always gets lots of compliments, especially considering what a snap it is to stir up! It's great alongside almost any protein, like Buttery Seared Scallops (page 168), or alongside the Brown Butter–Lemon Halibut with Asparagus and Olive Oil Whipped Potatoes (page 153) in place of the potatoes.

Line a plate with paper towels. Add the chopped bacon to a large cold Dutch oven or large pot with a lid and turn the heat to medium. Cook, stirring occasionally, until the bacon is browned and crispy, about 6 minutes. Leaving behind any browned bits and rendered fat in the pan, transfer the bacon to the paper towels to drain.

Add the peas and garlic to the Dutch oven. Sprinkle with the flour and cook, stirring constantly, about 2 minutes. Sprinkle in the garlic powder, paprika, salt, and pepper and cook, stirring frequently, until the peas begin to soften, about 5 minutes.

Stir in the chicken broth and half-and-half and bring to a boil. Stir in the pasta shells and bring back to a boil. Reduce the heat to low, cover, and simmer until the pasta is al dente, 8 to 10 minutes. Stir in the Parmesan.

Serve topped with crispy bacon and the thyme.

Major Mains / 183

Spinach and Cheddar–Stuffed Meatloaf with Extra Sauce

SERVES 6 / TOTAL TIME: 1 HOUR AND 15 MINUTES

1½ cups ketchup

1 tablespoon red wine vinegar

⅓ cup packed light brown sugar

2 pounds ground beef, 80% lean

½ yellow onion, grated or finely chopped

2 large eggs

½ cup Italian-style bread crumbs

1 teaspoon kosher salt

½ teaspoon freshly ground black pepper

6 ounces shredded cheddar cheese

3 cups spinach, coarsely chopped (baby or regular)

Olive Oil Whipped Potatoes (page 154), for serving (see Note)

I honestly didn't realize that meatloaf wasn't usually stuffed with anything because I grew up eating it the way my mom made it: stuffed with cheesy spinach and loaded with delicious sauce. Sounds pretty good, right? It just makes every other recipe seem boring once you've had it this way. My mom made this once a week when I was a kid and she still makes it for my dad on the reg. I recently whipped one up for a group of friends on a cold rainy night, served with a big scoop of mashed potatoes on the side, and it had everyone fighting for seconds and even thirds! Comfort food plus nostalgia is awfully hard to resist. It'll warm up a chilly night in the best possible way. My dad likes it extra saucy so that's how you're getting it, too. It's a large serving so it's ideal for leftovers (meatloaf sandwiches!!!) during the week. Serve with the Olive Oil Whipped Potatoes (page 154).

Preheat the oven to 425ºF.

Place a 12 x 13-inch piece of parchment paper on a work surface.

In a small bowl, combine the ketchup, vinegar, and brown sugar and set aside.

In a large bowl, combine the beef, onion, eggs, bread crumbs, salt, and pepper. Mix to incorporate. Transfer the mixture to the parchment paper and flatten into a 10 x 6-inch rectangle about ½ inch thick. Spread the cheddar and spinach over the meat, leaving about 1½-inches around the edges. With a short side facing you, use the parchment paper to help you lift and roll the meatloaf into a log. Remove the meatloaf from the parchment and place it seam-side down in a 9 x 5-inch loaf pan.

Bake for 20 minutes. Reduce the heat to 350ºF and bake for an additional 45 to 50 minutes; an instant-read thermometer inserted into the center of the meatloaf should read 160ºF. Remove the meatloaf from the oven and spread enough ketchup mixture to fully coat the top. Turn the oven to broil and broil until the top is dark burgundy in color, about 3 minutes.

Remove from the oven and let it rest 5 minutes. Top the meatloaf with another coat of the leftover ketchup mixture, and transfer the rested meatloaf to a cutting board and slice.

Serve on top of Olive Oil Whipped Potatoes (page 154) with a drizzle of any leftover sauce.

NOTE

You might want to make an extra half recipe of the potatoes to feed six.

SOUP QUEEN

I confess, I am That Girl. The one who orders a steaming hot bowl of soup at a restaurant in the dead of summer. But I will not apologize, because I am the Soup Queen! I'm all in, whether it's rich and decadent Soupe à l'Oignon (page 194), thick with gooey cheese, or my legendary Greek-Style Lemon Chicken Soup (page 205). And then there's Marry Me Chicken Chili (page 189), which earned me many fans and gave me my Brocc crown. Still not with me? Then how about Chicken Pot Pie Soup with Flaky Biscuits (page 190) or Cioppino Made Easy (page 193)? Okay, so maybe soup's not really so royal, but it is practical . . . a great way to empty the fridge, like in my recipe for nourishing Chickpea Noodle Soup (page 201). Light,

easy to make, really varied, and super versatile, plus soups store really well in the freezer for an easy lunch. Also, soup is great as a fun dinner party starter because it's already done before the guests arrive and can stay simmering on the stove, so you don't have to split your time between the kitchen and the party. Best of all, cleanup is painless (for my fellow dish haters) because you've only used one pot! Served with some warm bread, salad, wine, or drinks, you can't deny that soup is a perfect food!

Marry Me Chicken Chili

SERVES 6 / TOTAL TIME: 40 MINUTES

2 boneless, skinless, chicken breasts (6 to 8 ounces each)

1½ teaspoons kosher salt, plus more to taste

½ teaspoon freshly ground black pepper, plus more to taste

3 tablespoons extra-virgin olive oil

1 white onion, diced

4 garlic cloves, finely chopped

1 cup corn kernels, frozen or drained canned

2 (10-ounce) cans diced fire-roasted tomatoes with green chiles, undrained

2 cups chicken broth

1 (15-ounce) can black beans, drained and rinsed

1 (4½-ounce) can green chiles

2 teaspoons chili powder, plus more to taste

1 teaspoon ground cumin

1 teaspoon dried oregano

1 teaspoon sweet paprika

6 ounces cream cheese, cut into pieces, at room temperature (see Note)

2 cups roughly chopped curly kale leaves, midribs removed (from about 1 bunch)

TOPPINGS

4 green onions, thinly sliced

3 avocados, diced

2 cups whole-milk Greek yogurt or sour cream

2 cups shredded cheddar or Mexican blend cheese

Tortilla chips

This beloved recipe from my blog is responsible for not only its fair share of first-place chili cook-off ribbons but also more than a couple of marriage proposals. Seriously! I first noticed this chili had some magical powers when I started making it back in college. Every guy I ever made it for fell for me! I didn't think anything of it until I started receiving messages of similar stories. Since then, it has officially been renamed "Marry Me Chicken Chili" because it will seriously get you that ring. Use it wisely.

NOTE

The cream cheese must be at room temperature so that it doesn't curdle when you add it to the soup. My trick is to place it in a sealable bag and submerge it in warm water until it softens up.

Season the chicken breasts with ½ teaspoon of the salt and ½ teaspoon of the pepper.

Heat 2 tablespoons of olive oil in a Dutch oven or large pot over medium heat. Add the chicken breasts and cook for about 5 minutes per side (not cooked through; it will continue cooking in the chili). Set aside.

Add the remaining 1 tablespoon of the oil to the Dutch oven along with the onion and garlic and cook over medium heat, stirring occasionally, until the onion is slightly softened, 3 to 4 minutes. Stir in the corn and cook just to heat through, 30 seconds to 1 minute. Add the chicken, tomatoes, chicken

broth, beans, green chiles, chili powder, cumin, oregano, paprika, remaining 1 teaspoon of the salt, and a few twists of pepper and stir to combine.

Add the cream cheese pieces to the pot and stir to combine. Increase the heat to high and bring the mixture to a boil. Reduce the heat to low, cover, and simmer for 20 minutes.

Remove the chicken from the pot, shred or slice it, then return back to the pot. Stir in the kale, taste for salt and heat, and adjust to your taste. Add more chicken broth if you prefer a thinner chili.

Serve in a big pot with bowls and all the toppings.

Chicken Pot Pie Soup with Flaky Biscuits

SERVES 6 / TOTAL TIME: 40 MINUTES

SPECIAL EQUIPMENT: IMMERSION BLENDER

QUICK DROP BISCUITS

3 cups all-purpose flour

1 tablespoon baking powder

¼ teaspoon baking soda

½ teaspoon kosher salt

6 tablespoons cold unsalted butter, cut into small pieces

½ cup whole-milk Greek yogurt

½ cup whole milk

1 large egg

SOUP

2 skinless, boneless chicken breasts (6 to 8 ounces each)

1 teaspoon kosher salt

¼ teaspoon freshly ground black pepper

3 tablespoons extra-virgin olive oil

2 large carrots, peeled and diced

2 celery stalks, diced

1 yellow onion, diced

2 garlic cloves, finely chopped

2 cups diced peeled Yukon Gold potatoes (about 1 pound)

3 cups chicken broth

1½ cups milk, dairy or nondairy (oat or almond milk work great!)

2 teaspoons fresh thyme leaves

1 cup frozen peas

2 tablespoons grated Parmesan cheese, optional

Talk about comfort food! You know how much you love chicken pot pie? Okay, now imagine it as a delicious bowl of soup with some super easy biscuits on the side, because it wouldn't be a pot pie without a flaky, buttery crust! A last little touch of salty grated Parm puts it over the top in the best way, but feel free to leave it out for a dairy-free soup; same with swapping out whole milk for the unflavored oat or almond versions, you'll barely notice the difference. To make it really easy, feel free to use store-bought biscuits or try one of my favorite chicken soup hacks by using an already cooked rotisserie chicken! Shred the meat and make sure to add it in at the end so the chicken stays tender. For a full-on comfort night dinner don't forget a few squares of Salty, Crunchy Fudge (page 245).

Make the biscuits: Preheat the oven to 400°F. Line a sheet pan with parchment paper.

In a stand mixer fitted with a paddle (or in a bowl with a handheld mixer), beat together the flour, baking powder, baking soda, and salt on low until evenly combined, 10 to 20 seconds. Add the butter and mix until the mixture looks like coarse crumbs, about 1 minute. Do not overmix. Add the yogurt and milk and mix on low until a rough dough forms, 30 seconds to 1 minute. This will make rustic biscuits with craggy bits to catch the soup!

Remove the dough and gently gather it together enough to form drop biscuits. Using a large spoon, scoop 12 large dollops (about 2 tablespoons' worth) onto the sheet pan about 1 inch apart.

To make the egg wash, mix 1 tablespoon of water with the egg and, using a pastry brush, lightly brush the top of the biscuits with the egg wash. Bake until golden, about 12 minutes.

Make the soup: Season the chicken with ½ teaspoon of the kosher salt and the pepper.

Heat 2 tablespoons of olive oil in a Dutch oven or large pot over medium heat. Add the chicken and cook for 2 minutes on each side (not cooked through; it will cook more in the soup). Set the chicken on a plate.

Add the remaining 1 tablespoon of oil to the pot. Add the carrots, celery, onion, and garlic and cook, stirring occasionally, until the vegetables have softened, about 5 minutes. Add the potatoes, broth, milk, thyme,

remaining ½ teaspoon of the salt, and a few twists of the pepper and stir to combine. Return the chicken to the pot, increase the heat to high, and bring to a boil. Reduce the heat to low, cover, and simmer for 10 minutes.

Remove the chicken breasts and set aside. You can blend the soup with an immersion blender or with a stand blender. For an immersion blender, scoop out one-quarter of the soup and set aside. Then blend the soup in the pot until just slightly chunky. For a stand blender, blend in batches, blending all but one-quarter of the soup (be sure to open the steam vent in the blender lid). Combine the soups. Shred the chicken and add to the soup along with the peas. Stir until the peas are heated through, about 1 minute. If desired, stir in the Parmesan. Season to taste with salt and pepper and serve the soup with a plate of biscuits alongside.

Cioppino Made Easy

SERVES 4 / TOTAL TIME: 30 MINUTES

TOMATO BROTH

3 tablespoons extra-virgin olive oil

4 garlic cloves, chopped

2 large shallots, sliced

¼ cup roughly chopped fresh basil

2 teaspoons fresh oregano leaves

2 teaspoons fresh thyme leaves

2 teaspoons kosher salt

½ teaspoon freshly ground black pepper

¼ teaspoon red chile flakes

1 cup dry white wine, such as Sauvignon Blanc

1 (28-ounce) can peeled whole tomatoes (preferably San Marzano), undrained

SEAFOOD

1 pound skinless firm white fish, such as halibut, or cod, cut into 2-inch chunks

½ teaspoon kosher salt

¼ teaspoon freshly ground black pepper

½ pound mussels, scrubbed

½ pound shrimp, peeled, deveined, and tails removed

Chopped fresh parsley, for garnish

Cheesy Garlic Bread (without the Warm Marinara) (page 58) or any crusty bread

As much as I love cooking, there are some dishes I expected to only ever order in a restaurant, like cioppino. San Francisco's famous tomato-based seafood stew always seemed out of reach because it's complicated, not to mention expensive, with so many ingredients and different types of seafood. But one of the main goals of this book is to make those challenging recipes more approachable for you (and me), and after a few tries I finally cracked the code with this version. I simplified it a bit, narrowing the fish down to easily available types of seafood that aren't tricky to cook. I love to use halibut, but you can use cod, swordfish, and I've even used an assortment of fish cubes from the seafood counter (which tend to be very affordable). You can swap the mussels out for clams, add scallops or squid . . . you see where I'm going with this . . . totally customizable. You really can't go wrong! I've replaced the time-intensive seafood stock with a quick, herby tomato broth that cries out for a dunk with my Cheesy Garlic Bread (page 58—just hold the marinara). Even though I've tried to simplify cioppino, this still really is more of a special-occasion splurge-worthy soup that will deliver praise from your guests, in between slurps!

Make the tomato broth: Heat the olive oil in a large Dutch oven or large pot over medium heat. Add the garlic and shallots and cook, stirring until fragrant, about 2 minutes. Add the basil, oregano, thyme, salt, pepper, chile flakes, and stir to wilt the basil. Stir in the wine and simmer until reduced by about half, about 5 minutes. Add 5 cups of water and the tomatoes, crushing them with your hands as you add them, along with their liquid. Bring the broth to a boil, cover, and simmer on low heat for 30 minutes. (The broth can be made 3 to 4 days in advance and kept in an airtight container in the refrigerator.)

Add the seafood: Season the fish with salt and pepper and add to the broth. Stir in the mussels and shrimp, cover, and cook for 2 minutes. Stir, cover again, and check for doneness after another 2 to 3 minutes. The shrimp should be completely opaque and the mussel shells should be open. Remove from the heat, taste for additional salt and pepper.

Ladle the cioppino into bowls, making sure everyone gets some of the fish, mussels, and shrimp. Garnish with parsley and serve with the garlic bread or other crusty bread to soak up that delicious broth!

Soupe à l'Oignon (aka French Onion Soup)

SERVES 6 / TOTAL TIME: 1 HOUR 20 MINUTES

- 3 tablespoons unsalted butter
- 3 tablespoons extra-virgin olive oil
- 4 yellow onions, thinly sliced into half-moons
- ½ teaspoon kosher salt
- 2 garlic cloves, finely chopped
- 1 tablespoon all-purpose flour
- ½ cup white wine
- 6 cups beef broth
- 1 tablespoon Worcestershire sauce or soy sauce
- 1 tablespoon fresh thyme leaves
- Kosher salt, to taste
- Freshly ground black pepper, to taste
- 6 ½-inch thin long slices of French bread, cut on the diagonal
- 2 teaspoons extra-virgin olive oil
- 1 cup shredded Gruyère cheese
- Fresh thyme leaves for garnish

Soupe à l'oignon is definitely one of my top five all-time favorites. There's really nothing quite like dunking your spoon past that decadent layer of Gruyère to get a perfect bite of rich broth, caramelized onions, and cheesy toast. It's timeless, and for good reason. It's like the Little Black Dress of soups, perfect for every occasion—or like your favorite jeans, it never fails you. I lighten up the flavor of the traditional version by swapping the port wine for white wine, and add a shot of Worcestershire or soy sauce to replace the usual long-simmering classic French beef stock. If you can't find Gruyère, Jarlsberg or Emmentaler is a good substitute. This is rainy day, five-hundred-page novel, and red wine territory kind of soup that becomes a full meal when served alongside the Arugula Salad with Creamy White Beans and Basil Vinaigrette (page 100).

Melt the butter and olive oil in a Dutch oven or large pot over medium heat. Add the onions and salt and cook, stirring occasionally, until the onions are a rich caramel brown and extremely soft, 30 to 45 minutes. Trust me, it's worth the wait! If the onions begin to brown too quickly, reduce the heat, or if they do not begin to turn golden brown within 15 to 20 minutes, the heat is too low.

Stir in the garlic. Sprinkle with the flour and stir frequently for about 1 minute to toast the flour. Increase the heat to medium-high, add the wine, and use a wooden spoon or spatula to scrape up the browned bits stuck to the pot (this is deglazing a pan). Let the wine reduce for 2 to 3 minutes.

Increase the heat to high, add the broth, Worcestershire sauce, thyme, and salt and pepper and bring the soup to a boil. Reduce the heat to low, cover, and simmer for 30 minutes.

Preheat the oven to 400°F. Line a sheet pan with foil.

Brush both sides of the baguette slices with olive oil and place on the sheet pan. Bake until golden brown and crispy, 6 to 7 minutes, flipping the toasts over halfway through baking.

Preheat the broiler to high.

Ladle the soup into six 12-ounce broiler-proof bowls (see Note). Set the bowls on a sheet pan. Add the toasted bread and top with the Gruyère. Broil until the cheese turns golden brown, 2 to 3 minutes.

Top with the thyme and a few twists of pepper.

NOTES

If you don't have broiler-proof bowls, you can top the bread slices with the cheese, set on a sheet pan, and broil them to melt the cheese. Then serve the soup in regular bowls, with a cheese toast on top. Another option is to top the bread with cheese and set them in the whole soup pot and pop that in the oven. Just double-check that your pot is ovenproof, of course! Please don't skip this part!

To make this vegetarian, use vegetable broth instead of beef broth, and use a vegan Worcestershire sauce, increasing the amount to 2 tablespoons.

Spicy Lasagna Soup

SERVES 4 / TOTAL TIME: 40 MINUTES

LASAGNA SOUP

- 1 tablespoon extra-virgin olive oil
- 1 yellow onion, chopped
- 2 garlic cloves, finely chopped
- ½ pound ground beef, preferably 85% lean
- ½ pound sweet Italian sausage, casings removed
- 2 tablespoons tomato paste
- ½ tablespoon crushed Calabrian chile peppers in oil or 1 teaspoon red chile flakes
- 1 tablespoon Italian seasoning
- ½ teaspoon kosher salt
- ½ teaspoon freshly ground black pepper
- 1 (24-ounce) jar marinara sauce (preferably Rao's)
- 4 cups chicken broth
- 8 ounces lasagna noodles, broken into small pieces (think the size of your spoon!)

CHEESE TOPPING

- 8 ounces ricotta cheese
- ½ cup shredded mozzarella cheese
- 2 tablespoons grated Parmesan cheese, plus more for serving
- ½ teaspoon kosher salt
- ½ teaspoon freshly ground black pepper
- 2 to 3 tablespoons finely chopped fresh parsley, for garnish

I'm usually not one to mess with perfection, but I've always thought lasagna was *begging* to be made into a soup. A slice of lasagna is like a cheesy layered hug, and my soup version totally delivers on the flavor and coziness without the time-consuming mess of layering noodles and sauce and cheese. The hug arrives in one pot and comes together in just 40 minutes. It gets a boost from one of my fave ingredients, Calabrian chile peppers. They're medium-spicy and a little bit sweet, a perfect combination—though feel free to use a little crushed red pepper flakes if you'd prefer. For those who are sensitive to spice, you can totally leave it out or start with a small quantity. You can always add more spice, but you can't take it away! If you're out of lasagna noodles there's nothing wrong with subbing in an equal amount of whatever dried pasta you have on hand, like penne or manicotti (broken up). Just make sure to adjust the timing, since lasagna noodles take longer to cook than most other pastas.

Make the lasagna soup: Heat the oil in a Dutch oven or large soup pot over medium heat. Add the onion and garlic and cook, stirring, until the onion is golden, about 5 minutes.

Add the beef and sausage and cook, breaking up the meat into smaller pieces with a wooden spoon or spatula and stirring occasionally, until the meat is browned, 5 to 7 minutes.

With a large metal spoon, carefully remove and discard all but 1 tablespoon of fat from the pot. Add the tomato paste, chiles, Italian seasoning, salt, and pepper and stir until well combined, about 1 minute. Increase the heat to high, add the marinara sauce, chicken broth, and 1 cup of water, bring to a boil, then reduce the heat and simmer for 10 minutes. Stir in the lasagna noodles, cover, reduce the heat to low, and simmer until the noodles are al dente, soft, but slightly firm, 10 to 15 minutes. If you prefer a very brothy soup, add an additional ½ to 1 cup of hot broth.

Meanwhile, make the cheese topping: In a small bowl, combine the ricotta, mozzarella, Parmesan, salt, and pepper. Set aside until the soup is done.

Ladle into individual bowls and top each with a generous scoop of the cheese topping and some fresh parsley. Pass the Parmesan at the table!

NOTE: Add additional chicken broth or water if you prefer a thinner soup.

Golden Cauliflower Soup

SERVES 4 / TOTAL TIME: 35 MINUTES
SPECIAL EQUIPMENT: IMMERSION BLENDER

ROASTED CAULIFLOWER

4 cups cauliflower florets (about 1¼ pounds)

3 tablespoons extra-virgin olive oil

2 teaspoons ground turmeric

1 teaspoon ground cumin

1 teaspoon kosher salt

½ teaspoon red chile flakes, optional

½ teaspoon freshly ground black pepper

SOUP

2 tablespoons extra-virgin olive oil

1 yellow onion, chopped

2 garlic cloves, finely chopped

1 large sweet potato, peeled and cubed (about 2 cups)

4 cups vegetable broth

1 can (13½ ounces) full-fat coconut milk

TOASTED PUMPKIN SEEDS

⅓ cup pumpkin seeds

½ tablespoon extra-virgin olive oil

½ teaspoon garlic powder

½ teaspoon kosher salt

Freshly ground black pepper

Finely chopped fresh parsley or cilantro, for garnish

I wanted to make a super-healthy soup that would be the perfect antidote to a long weekend (feel-good food vibes, you know?), and was expecting it to be a bit of a chore to eat—I had no idea it was going to deliver like this crave-worthy cauliflower soup does. Not only is it basically all veggies, kicked up with my favorite anti-inflammatory spice, turmeric, it's a warm cup (or in my case, bowl!) of soul. This soup is extra flexible, so change the ratio of cauli-flower to potato if that's what you're feeling. Same with the broth vs. coconut milk, if you prefer your soup lighter or creamier. Spice is the flavor dial that's always in your control, so crank it up or back it off. This freezes beautifully (without the pumpkin seeds, which you add after heating).

Roast the cauliflower: Preheat the oven to 425°F. Line a sheet pan with foil.

Arrange the cauliflower on the lined pan. Drizzle with the olive oil and sprinkle with the turmeric, cumin, salt, chile flakes (if using), and pepper and toss until evenly coated. (I use my hands, but be careful because turmeric will stain them. You can also do this in a bowl with a spatula and transfer to the pan.)

Roast for 20 minutes, tossing halfway through. Set the cauliflower aside after roasting. Reserve a few florets for garnish separately.

Leave the oven on, but reduce the temperature to 350°F (for the pumpkin seeds).

Make the soup: Heat the olive oil in a Dutch oven or large pot over medium heat. Add the onion and garlic and cook, stirring occasionally, until the onion is translucent, 5 to 7 minutes.

Add the sweet potato, vegetable broth, coconut milk, and roasted cauliflower. Increase the heat to high and bring to a boil. Reduce the heat to low, cover, and simmer until the sweet potatoes are soft, about 15 minutes.

Meanwhile, toast the pumpkin seeds: When the oven temperature reaches 350°F, spread the pumpkin seeds on the same sheet pan used for the cauliflower. Sprinkle with the olive oil, garlic powder, salt, and a few twists of pepper. Toss and bake until the seeds are toasted, about 12 minutes, tossing the seeds halfway through baking.

Finish the soup: With an immersion blender (or in small batches in a stand blender with the steam vent in the lid open), blend the soup until smooth.

Serve topped with the toasted pumpkin seeds and garnish with the reserved cauliflower florets and parsley or cilantro.

Chickpea Noodle Soup

SERVES 6 / TOTAL TIME: 20 MINUTES

3 tablespoons extra-virgin olive oil

3 carrots, peeled and chopped

2 celery stalks, chopped

1 yellow onion, chopped

4 garlic cloves, finely chopped

1-inch piece fresh ginger, peeled and grated

2 (15-ounce) cans chickpeas, drained and rinsed

8 cups chicken broth (or vegetable if you want to go all-veggie)

3 tablespoons finely chopped fresh parsley

2 tablespoons finely chopped fresh dill

1 tablespoon finely chopped fresh thyme leaves

1 teaspoon kosher salt

½ teaspoon freshly ground black pepper

8 ounces egg noodles (not wide)

Juice of 1 lemon

Who knew chicken noodle soup doesn't really need any chicken? Scandalous, I know, but here's something even more outrageous: I actually prefer mine *without*. Hear me out. I have nothing against traditional chicken noodle soup if that's your thing, but when I'm under the weather there's no way I'm handling raw chicken or spending more than twenty minutes cooking *anything*. So, you can see why I needed to mess with the original . . . and my take on it turned out to be the comforting cure-all that I was looking for—and that's really the point of this soup, right? Plus, since there's no protein to be cooked, you can have this ready in no time. And to throw you carnivores a bone, if you really feel my version is lacking you can totally add a couple of cups of cooked shredded chicken in instead of the chickpeas—or along with them even. I won't be insulted.

Heat the olive oil in a Dutch oven or large soup pot over medium heat. Add the carrots, celery, onion, garlic, and ginger and cook, stirring occasionally, until the vegetables begin to soften, 5 to 7 minutes.

Add the chickpeas, broth, parsley, dill, thyme, salt, and pepper and stir to combine. Increase the heat to high and bring to a boil. Stir in the egg noodles, reduce the heat to medium-low, cover, and simmer until the noodles are cooked, about 12 minutes.

Remove from the heat, and stir in the lemon juice and additional salt or pepper as desired.

Hungarian Mushroom Soup

SERVES 4 / TOTAL TIME: 30 MINUTES

2 tablespoons unsalted butter

2 tablespoons extra-virgin olive oil

1 pound mushrooms, a mix of baby bella (cremini) and white mushrooms, sliced

1 yellow onion, chopped

2 garlic cloves, finely chopped

2 tablespoons all-purpose flour

2 teaspoons Hungarian sweet paprika

2 teaspoons finely chopped fresh thyme leaves

1 teaspoon dried dill or 2 teaspoons finely chopped fresh

½ teaspoon kosher salt

½ teaspoon freshly ground black pepper

3 cups chicken or vegetable broth

¾ cup half-and-half

2 tablespoons reduced-sodium soy sauce

3 tablespoons sour cream, plus more (optional) for serving

Juice of ½ lemon

Finely chopped fresh parsley, for garnish

When you're craving something super savory and rich, this is the bowl for you. If you're already a mushroom lover, your life is about to be changed forever. And if you're not, this is the perfect dish to change your mind. When I was testing this recipe, some of the mushroom haters I know tried it—a bit reluctantly, granted—and were converted! I almost called it Magic Mushroom Soup, but I didn't want people to get the wrong idea (ha-ha)! The "Hungarian" aspect is the sweet paprika used here, and if you can find the legit item at the store, it will make a big difference. But regular spice-aisle paprika will work, too. And while I love smoked paprika (aka Spanish pimenton) and hot paprika, that is not what you want to use here. The baby bella (aka cremini) mushrooms have a slightly deeper flavor than regular white button ones if you can find them, but any mushroom—or a mixture of different shrooms—will work in this recipe.

Melt the butter and the olive oil in a Dutch oven or large pot over medium heat. Add the mushrooms, onion, and garlic and cook, stirring occasionally, until the mushrooms are softened, 10 to 12 minutes.

Sprinkle in the flour, paprika, thyme, dill, salt, and pepper and cook, stirring constantly, until the flour is lightly toasted, 30 seconds to 1 minute. Add the broth, half-and-half, and soy sauce and stir. Increase the heat and bring the soup to a boil. Reduce the heat to low, cover, and simmer for 15 minutes.

Remove from the heat and stir in the sour cream and lemon juice. Taste and adjust for salt and pepper. Serve with fresh parsley to garnish. You can also add a dollop of sour cream for additional creaminess.

Greek-Style Lemon Chicken Soup

SERVES 6 / TOTAL TIME: 30 MINUTES

2 boneless, skinless chicken breasts (about 8 ounces each)

1½ teaspoons kosher salt

¼ teaspoon freshly ground black pepper, plus more to taste

3 tablespoons extra-virgin olive oil, plus more for drizzling

2 carrots, peeled and diced

1 yellow onion, diced

3 garlic cloves, finely chopped

1 cup cauliflower rice or ½ cup uncooked orzo

2 tablespoons finely chopped fresh dill, plus more for garnish

2 tablespoons finely chopped fresh parsley, plus more for garnish

1 teaspoon dried oregano or 1 tablespoon finely chopped fresh

8 cups chicken broth

3 large egg yolks

Juice of 2 lemons

NOTE

If you used orzo and have leftovers, you may need to add more broth when reheating, as the orzo will have soaked up a lot of the original broth.

The most popular recipe on IG and my blog is a soup! Definitely didn't see that coming. Though I guess I'm not too surprised that this tart and chickeny soup would have its fans. The Greek name for the soup is *avgolemono*, and it's a lemony, dill-flavored chicken soup that's creamy without a drop of cream. The silky texture comes from gently blending egg yolks with hot broth, a really cool technique. Don't skip that part! It sounds harder than it actually is. Traditionally made with orzo, my version is also great with cauliflower rice if you'd prefer it vegetable-forward. For a complete dinner serve the Moroccan-Spiced Carrots with Whipped Feta (page 54). So light yet satisfying, it's a soup that's perfect year-round, or anytime you want to transport yourself to Greece!

Season the chicken with ½ teaspoon of the salt and the black pepper. Heat 2 tablespoons of the olive oil in a Dutch oven or large pot over medium heat. Add the chicken and cook until lightly golden brown, 2 minutes on each side (not cooked through; it will cook more in the soup). Set the chicken on a plate.

Add the remaining 1 tablespoon of oil to the pot along with the carrots, onion, and garlic. Season with 1 teaspoon salt and a few twists of pepper and cook, stirring occasionally, until the onion begins to brown, 5 to 7 minutes.

Stir in the cauliflower rice (but not the orzo if using, as this will go in later because it cooks faster), dill, parsley, and oregano. Add the chicken broth and return the chicken to the pot.

Bring the soup to a boil, cover, and reduce the heat to low and simmer for 15 minutes. Check that the chicken is fully cooked and remove it from the pot. If using orzo, add to the soup and continue simmering until the orzo is al dente, 7 to 9 minutes. When the chicken is cool enough to handle, shred it and then return it to the pot.

In a medium bowl, whisk the egg yolks. Remove 1 cup of hot broth in a spouted measuring cup and slowly pour the hot broth, about 1 tablespoon at a time, into the egg yolks while whisking vigorously, to prevent the eggs from scrambling. Whisk this warmed egg mixture into the soup pot. Stir in the lemon juice and adjust to your taste for salt and pepper.

Serve garnished with fresh parsley and dill and drizzle with a little olive oil!

Split Pea Soup with Crispy Sausage

SERVES 6 / TOTAL TIME: 1 HOUR
SPECIAL EQUIPMENT: IMMERSION BLENDER

4 tablespoons extra-virgin olive oil

1 yellow onion, diced

3 carrots, peeled and diced

3 celery stalks, diced

3 garlic cloves, peeled

1 Yukon Gold potato, peeled and cut into ½-inch chunks

1 pound dried green split peas, rinsed

8 cups vegetable or chicken broth

1 pound fully cooked chicken sausage (preferably Seemore brand) or kielbasa, thinly sliced on the diagonal

1 tablespoon fresh thyme leaves

2 teaspoons kosher salt, plus more to taste

1 teaspoon freshly ground black pepper, plus more to taste

Chopped fresh parsley, for garnish

This is a childhood favorite of mine (and maybe yours) that made the transition into adulthood. I associate it with the holidays, since it's traditionally made with a ham bone. A long-cooked bone is a classic flavoring addition and a way to use the last of the holiday ham. So rather than having this just around the holidays, I came up with this smoky meat-optional version, and I think it's just as good, sans ham. Not only are split peas super hearty, but they're a great source of protein.

It's also one of my favorite soups to make and freeze for weekday lunches! Just crisp up some sausage in a pan to top the soup and you have yourself a healthy, wholesome meal.

Heat 3 tablespoons of the olive oil in a large Dutch oven or soup pot over medium heat. Add the onion, carrots, and celery and cook, stirring occasionally, until the vegetables are soft, about 5 minutes. Add the garlic and potato and stir until the garlic is fragrant, about 1 minute. Stir in the split peas and add 1 cup of water and the broth. Increase the heat and bring the soup to a boil. Reduce the heat to low, cover, and simmer, stirring occasionally, until the peas are softened, about 30 minutes.

Uncover and continue to simmer, occasionally stirring and scraping the bottom of the pot to prevent sticking, until the peas are fully soft, about 15 minutes.

With an immersion blender (or in small batches in a stand blender with the steam vent in the lid open), blend the soup until smooth. I prefer a thick soup, but add additional stock or water if you'd like it looser, it's totally your preference!

Heat the remaining 1 tablespoon of olive oil in a medium skillet over medium heat. Add the sausage in one even layer so the slices do not overlap. Cook until the sausage is browned and crispy on both sides, 2 to 3 minutes per side. Stir in the thyme, salt, and pepper and adjust the seasonings as desired.

Ladle into individual bowls, garnish with fresh parsley, and top with the crispy sausage.

Red Wine Beef Stew

SERVES 6 / TOTAL TIME: 3½ HOURS

- 2 pounds beef stewing meat/chuck roast, fat trimmed off and cut into 1-inch cubes
- 2 teaspoons kosher salt
- ½ teaspoon freshly ground black pepper
- 2 tablespoons avocado oil, plus more if needed
- 3 tablespoons balsamic vinegar
- 1 yellow onion, sliced
- 4 garlic cloves, finely chopped
- 1 shallot, finely chopped
- 2 tablespoons tomato paste
- 2 tablespoons ketchup
- 2 tablespoons tapioca starch, cornstarch, or all-purpose flour
- 5 cups beef broth
- 1 cup red wine
- 2 bay leaves
- 2 tablespoons finely chopped fresh thyme or 1 teaspoon dried thyme
- 1 teaspoon dried oregano
- 3 large carrots, peeled and cut into 1-inch pieces
- 3 Yukon Gold potatoes, peeled and cut into 1-inch pieces
- 3 tablespoons chopped fresh parsley, for garnish
- Crusty bread, for serving

I make this insane beef stew every year during the holidays and I'm happy to say a lot of my Broccolinis have adopted the tradition, too, since I first posted this recipe on my Instagram a few years back. Although it is a bit time-consuming, it's basically foolproof. It's also perfect for hosting during the holiday season because you can do all of the chopping and searing before your guests arrive, so you can hang out and make cocktails while it braises into tender perfection in the oven. Plus, it's a full meal in itself, so you won't have to stress about sides! The meat comes out so tender you can cut it with a spoon! Make sure to have a couple loaves of fresh crusty bread on hand to soak up all that rich broth. By the way, waiting for a holiday is totally up to you. This is a comfort-food home run that works for cold weather or just any old Sunday night, whatever the temperature. Yum!

Preheat the oven to 325°F.

In a bowl, toss the beef with 1½ teaspoon of the salt and all of the pepper to coat all sides.

Heat the avocado oil in a large Dutch oven or other ovenproof pot with a lid over medium-high heat. Working in batches to not crowd the pan, cook the meat until well browned and crusted on all sides, about 3 minutes per side. If you overcrowd the pan, the meat will steam and not brown! Set the beef aside on a plate. Continue until all the meat has been browned, adding a tablespoon of additional oil to each batch of meat, if needed.

Add the vinegar to the pot and use a wooden spoon or spatula to scrape up the browned bits stuck to the bottom (this is deglazing the pan). Stir in the onion, garlic, and shallot, reduce the heat to medium, and cook, stirring occasionally, until the onion slices are translucent, 6 to 7 minutes. Stir in the tomato paste and ketchup and keep stirring and scraping the bottom of the pan to prevent sticking.

Add the beef with any accumulated juices to the pan. Sprinkle with the tapioca starch and stir the beef mixture for 1 minute to toast the starch. Add the beef broth, red wine, bay leaves, thyme, oregano, remaining ½ teaspoon of the salt, and a few twists of pepper and stir to combine.

Bring the stew to a boil, cover, place in the oven, and bake for 1½ hours. Add the carrots and potatoes and cook until the meat is tender, about 1 hour. Discard the bay leaves. Taste and season with additional salt and pepper, if needed.

Serve garnished with parsley and with crusty bread to soak up the amazing sauce!

Pantry Tomato Soup with Puff Pastry

SERVES 4 / TOTAL TIME: 45 MINUTES
SPECIAL EQUIPMENT: IMMERSION BLENDER

PANTRY TOMATO SOUP

- 3 tablespoons extra-virgin olive oil
- 1 small yellow onion, chopped
- 3 garlic cloves, finely chopped
- 1 (28-ounce) can diced tomatoes, undrained
- 1½ cups chicken or vegetable broth
- 3 tablespoons chopped fresh basil or 1 teaspoon dried basil
- 2 tablespoons tomato paste
- 1 teaspoon kosher salt
- ½ teaspoon freshly ground black pepper
- ⅓ cup heavy cream

PUFF PASTRY TOPPING

- All-purpose flour, for dusting
- 1 sheet of frozen puff pastry, thawed
- 1 large egg, beaten
- Flaky sea salt, for garnish

Soup for me is almost always linked to a comforting memory, like when my mom used to take my sister and me down to Crystal Cove in Laguna Beach for lunch at our favorite beachfront restaurant. My standing order was tomato soup with puff pastry on top, served piping hot. It always hit the spot on a chilly day at the beach. Chances are you can make this soup with what's already in your pantry, as long as you have frozen puff pastry on hand (I always do). Of course, if you'd prefer, you can leave off the puff pastry—but it's such a fun update from tomato soup's traditional grilled cheese sidekick. Serve the soup in individual bowls or lay the entire puff pastry over a big bowl for a crowd. This soup freezes beautifully (right next to the puff pastry!), so you can access that cozy memory anytime.

Preheat the oven to 400°F. Line a sheet pan with foil.

Make the pantry tomato soup: Heat the olive oil in a large Dutch oven or large soup pot over medium heat. Add the onion and garlic and cook, stirring occasionally, until the onion is translucent, 5 to 7 minutes.

Add the diced tomatoes and their juices, broth, basil, tomato paste, salt, and pepper and stir to combine. Bring the soup to a boil. Reduce the heat to low, cover, and simmer for 15 minutes.

With an immersion blender (or in small batches in a stand blender with the steam vent in the lid open), blend the soup until smooth. Mix in the heavy cream and taste for additional salt and pepper as needed.

Make the puff pastry topping: Ladle the soup into 4 10-ounce ovenproof bowls. Set the bowls on the foil-lined sheet pan. Place the puff pastry on a piece of parchment paper or a work surface lightly dusted with flour. With a knife, cut out 4 rounds ½ to 1 inch wider in diameter than the top of the soup bowl (you want a ¼ to ½ inch overhang all around). Brush the edges of the bowls with the beaten egg and place a puff pastry round on top of each bowl. Pinch the edges of the puff pastry to the rim of the bowl to seal closed. Brush the top of the pastry with the beaten egg wash.

Slide the sheet pan into the oven and bake until the puff pastry is golden brown, 12 to 14 minutes.

Serve sprinkled with some flaky sea salt.

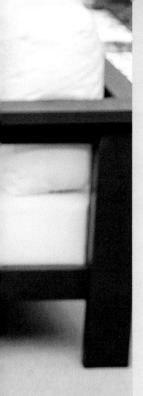

CHEERS TO THAT

My life is ever-changing, but if there's one thing that's stayed consistent over the last few years, it's my love for amazing food and great cocktails. I don't discriminate, I love my margs, mules, spritzes, Negronis, slushies, smashes, you name it. In this chapter, I'm breaking down the recipes for ten of my very favorite cocktails—classic, delicious, and exciting drinks for any occasion. Fun libations that come in many forms and flavors, from fruity to spicy and even briny. I pride myself on making a well-balanced cocktail that has just enough of a kick from alcohol but still lets the other flavors have their say as well. You'll find the few bar tools you need to make these drinks in Kitchen Essentials (page 23). They're very standard; the one you might have to buy is a muddler because I find gently mashing berries, herbs, and citrus is the secret to a well-flavored drink, but honestly the end of a wooden spoon will do! I stick to the bar basics here and leave the fancy liquors behind, never use too much sugar, and always have fun. And what's a cocktail without a fabulous meal? So throughout the book I've suggested dishes that partner well with different drinks. Juicy and refreshing, most are also easy to turn into mocktails if that's your thing. Cheers to that!

Tequila Negroni

MAKES 4 COCKTAILS / TOTAL TIME: 10 MINUTES

Ice

4 ounces tequila (you can use gin for a classic Negroni)

4 ounces Campari

4 ounces sweet red vermouth

1 large ice cube for the finished cocktail

Orange twists, for garnish

If you're looking for a classic cocktail with a touch of Italian sophistication, you can't do better than the Negroni. It's the cobblestone streets of Florence, on ice, with a twist. Spirit-heavy and slightly bitter thanks to the versatile aperitif Campari, it's traditionally made with gin but that can be swapped out for any liquor to suit your mood. I am a tequila girl through and through, so this is my preferred recipe. A perfect cocktail to make in a big batch for friends and a great way to discover Campari if you're not acquainted yet, mixed with a little or a lot of soda water for the lighter drinkers in your crew. Great to serve with Balsamic Skirt Steak with Chimichurri and Blistered Tomatoes (page 160), or many of the apps in the book, especially the Marinated Olives and Manchego (page 41).

In an ice-filled mixing glass, combine the tequila, Campari, and vermouth and stir until the mixture is cold, about 30 seconds. Strain into 4 chilled rocks or old-fashioned glasses with the ice cube (or straight up, if you prefer) and garnish with an orange twist.

VARIATION:

For something less spirited, swap the tequila for 8 ounces of prosecco to make a Negroni Sbagliato.

Lavender Haze

MAKES 2 COCKTAILS / TOTAL TIME: 35 MINUTES (INCLUDES 30 MINUTES FOR LAVENDER SYRUP)

4 ounces gin (preferably Empress 1908 Indigo)

1 ounce fresh lemon juice

1 ounce Lavender Simple Syrup (recipe follows)

Ice

6 ounces tonic water or club soda

2 fresh lavender sprigs, for garnish

You will be giving off top-shelf mixologist vibes when you shake up one of these elegant cocktails dedicated to my girl, Taylor Swift (named after her song "Lavender Haze"). I think Taylor would appreciate the sophisticated, delicately floral lavender plus the gorgeous purple color and juniper bite that you get from Empress gin. Of course, gin is not naturally purple, but Empress has blue butterfly pea flowers, and when the acid from the lemon juice mixes with the flowers the color becomes a magical lavender. (But try this with any gin you have!) This is a truly Insta-worthy drink—just don't forget to put *Midnights* on repeat. The lavender syrup alone is enough to make it worth your while, adding depth to a morning iced latte or elevating a simple iced tea. Just don't go foraging in your local park for the lavender: Make sure you source the culinary-grade variety (I order it online). This fragrant drink goes "All Too Well" with fish dishes like Pistachio Pesto Salmon (page 112) or Mediterranean Fish in Parchment with Perfect Stovetop Rice (page 83), or even Chicken Satay and Kale Salad (page 98).

In a small pitcher or measuring cup, stir together the gin, lemon juice, and Lavender Simple Syrup. Pour into 2 ice-filled Collins glasses and top each drink with tonic water. Garnish with the lavender.

Lavender Simple Syrup

MAKES 1½ CUPS / TOTAL TIME: 30 MINUTES

1 cup water

1 cup sugar

3 tablespoons dried culinary lavender

In a medium saucepan, combine the water, sugar, and lavender and bring to a simmer over medium heat and simmer for 10 minutes. Remove from the heat, cover, and allow the lavender to infuse the syrup for 15 to 20 minutes. The longer the mixture steeps, the stronger the flavor. Strain the syrup into a mason jar or sealable container and keep refrigerated for up to 2 weeks if not using immediately.

Spicy Rosé Spritz

SERVES 8 / TOTAL TIME: 5 MINUTES

Ice

1 (750 ml) bottle dry rosé (not too sweet), chilled

8 lime wedges

1 (16-ounce) bottle sparkling water

1 to 2 jalapeños, thinly sliced, for garnish

This spritz literally describes me as a person. It's simple, refreshing, and a little spicy, which is probably how I would market myself on a dating app. I love this spicy spritz because it's always fun to serve your guests something that slightly surprises them. If you want extra spice, you can muddle the jalapeño in the bottom of your glass before you add the rest of the ingredients. You can also make pitchers of these ahead of time for a party and wait to add the sparkling water right before serving. My friends and I will drink these in the backyard all day, all summer long. It's just the thing when you want to day drink and still make it out for dinner at night (something I haven't done since turning thirty, but let a girl reminisce)!

For each spritz, add ice to a wineglass, pour 3 ounces of rosé into the glass, add a squeeze of lime, top off with a splash of sparkling water, garnish with 2 or 3 jalapeño slices, and enjoy!

Aperol Slushie

MAKES 4 COCKTAILS / TOTAL TIME: 10 MINUTES, PLUS 3 HOURS FREEZING TIME

1½ cups prosecco (preferably La Marca)

1 cup Aperol

1 cup water

Orange slices, for garnish

If enjoying an Aperol spritz on a summer afternoon is basic, then I'm proud to be basic. I just can't think of a better summer drink. But you know me, I'm always experimenting, so I messed with it a bit and turned it into a slushie! Not bad for a basic B, huh? They're really fun to drink and totally memorable, but the best part is how easily they come together and how quickly they raise the vibe of your backyard party. I always end up doubling the recipe because even the macho beer drinkers will ditch their cans for a cute little slushie! Serve with Famous Beverly Hills Chopped Salad (page 125) and Cioppino Made Easy (page 193) or Spicy Tuna Crispy Rice (page 144).

In a large pitcher or measuring cup, stir together the prosecco, Aperol, and water. Pour into an 8-inch square baking pan and freeze for 3 hours or overnight. Let the pan sit out for 1 to 2 minutes, then slide a knife around the edge to loosen the ice. Carefully cut into large chunks. In either a blender or food processor pulse the chunks once or twice into a slush. Transfer to 4 big wineglasses and garnish with an orange slice.

Vodka Watermelon Spritz

MAKES 2 COCKTAILS / TOTAL TIME: 5 MINUTES

3 to 4 mint leaves, plus 2 sprigs for garnish

½ ounce lime juice

Ice

4 ounces vodka (tequila works, too, of course *wink*)

4 ounces watermelon juice (store-bought or about 1 cup cubed watermelon, blended; I never strain)

1 to 2 ounces Simple Syrup, to taste (recipe follows)

Sparkling water

NOTE

I make my own watermelon juice by blending fresh watermelon but you can use store-bought.

If ever there was a vacation in a glass, this Vodka Watermelon Spritz is it. Fruity, not too sweet, refreshing, and invigorating . . . just like a weekend out of town! Plus, it's totally photo-ready when you feel like your IG feed has been a little lacking. I made it with watermelon because the red-pink color is the stamp on your passport to paradise, but try a yellow watermelon, a honeydew, or why not a cantaloupe . . . they're all beautiful as long as they're ripe and at the peak of flavor. Whether it's a Tuesday after work or a weekend afternoon, it's always a hit. You can even bottle it up and throw it in your bag to accompany you on a real getaway!

In a cocktail shaker, use a muddler or the end of a wooden spoon to muddle the mint and lime juice. Add the ice, vodka, watermelon juice, and 1 ounce of Simple Syrup and shake well. Taste and add more Simple Syrup as needed depending on the sweetness of your watermelon. Strain into 2 ice-filled glasses (the size of the glass depends on how spritzy you're feeling—for a lighter drink, reach for a taller glass!) and top off with sparkling water. Garnish with a sprig of mint.

Simple Syrup

MAKES 1½ CUPS / TOTAL TIME: 10 MINUTES

1 cup sugar

1 cup water

In a small saucepan combine the sugar and the water and bring the mixture to a boil until the sugar has completely dissolved. Remove from the heat and allow the mixture to cool. Store in a mason jar or sealed container in the refrigerator for up to 2 weeks

Dirty Martini with Blue Cheese Olives

MAKES 4 COCKTAILS / TOTAL TIME: 10 MINUTES

BLUE CHEESE OLIVES

**3 ounces blue cheese,
at room temperature**

**3 ounces cream cheese,
at room temperature**

1 teaspoon milk

**12 pitted green olives (I use
Spanish martini olives),
drained, brine reserved**

MARTINIS

**10 ounces gin or vodka
(preferably Hendrick's Gin or
Tito's Handmade Vodka)**

2 ounces dry vermouth

**2 ounces olive brine (reserved
from the olives)**

Does this sound like you? There's something you really, *really* want to like, but try as you might you just don't click with it? The aspiration remains because it looks so good and you vow to keep trying until you force it to become your thing, too. For me, it's the dirty martini. I will never stop trying to be a dirty martini girl even though, honestly, I can't do more than a sip. Sad, yes, but I wasn't about to take no for an answer. The blue cheese–stuffed olives are what do it for me. The strong briny, salty blast you get from them takes this dirty to a whole new place. Look for Spanish martini olives that are already pitted and remove the pimiento—or keep it if you like! You want to shake this cocktail like mad and serve it arctic cold, with those beautiful little shards of ice floating on the surface. Martini fanatics and purists insist you shake these one at a time. By now you know I'm not a martini fanatic so I make mine two at a time, but feel free! For all you cool, mysterious martini lovers, enjoy this one. I envy you and will never stop trying to be like you. Honestly, I still haven't managed to finish a whole one of these yet, but that day is coming, I promise you! And of course, while this is perfect with either Major Main steak recipe (pages 156 and 160), it's pretty cocktail-party glam with Stuffed Mushroom Dip (page 49), too.

Make the blue cheese olives: If your cheeses are soft enough, you can use a wooden spoon and some arm power to stir them together along with the milk to make a smooth blend. If not, use an electric mixer or a small food processor and do more dishes! Transfer the cheese mixture to a piping bag fitted with a small tip (or even simpler a plastic bag with the corner cut out) and pipe the cheese into the olives. Set aside.

Make the martinis: Add ice and water to 4 martini glasses to chill them while you make the cocktails. Make 2 martinis at a time. In an ice-filled cocktail shaker, combine 5 ounces gin, 1 ounce vermouth, and 1 ounce olive brine and shake vigorously until ice cold, at least 10 seconds. Empty the ice and water out of the 2 chilled glasses and strain the martinis into the glasses. Garnish each with 3 blue cheese olives. Repeat to make 1 more batch of martinis.

La Vaquera

MAKES 2 COCKTAILS / TOTAL TIME: 35 MINUTES

CHOCOLATE-ORANGE GARNISH

¼ cup semisweet chocolate chips

1 teaspoon coconut oil

2 dried orange slices (about 2 inches in diameter)

COCKTAILS

Ice (see Note)

8 ounces freshly squeezed orange juice

4 ounces mezcal (I prefer Madre Mezcal, plus it looks cute on a bar cart)

12 shakes Angostura bitters

8 shakes chocolate bitters (or 6 shakes Angostura bitters)

NOTE

If you are making multiple cocktails, add fresh ice to the shaker as needed before shaking each one.

Meet the cowgirl! She's a little wild and a little more to wrangle than a margarita, but definitely worth the effort. This cocktail takes you on a sunset ride through a range of flavors including the smoke of mezcal, the sweet and sour of freshly squeezed OJ, and the surprising note of chocolate from the bitters made with cacao. Since I can't get enough of chocolate and orange, I added a chocolate-dipped orange wagon wheel garnish! This cocktail takes a bit more shopping and planning than most of the other sips in this book, but it's easy to order the chocolate bitters online, and if you can't find them, add a few extra shakes of the Angostura bitters. Pair her with the Elote Nachos (page 38). *Salud!*

Make the chocolate-orange garnish: Line a plate with parchment paper.

In a small microwave-safe bowl, combine the chocolate chips and coconut oil and microwave at 50 percent power in 20- to 30-second increments, stirring well after each, until completely melted and smooth, 40 seconds to 1 minute total.

Dip half of 1 dried orange slice in the melted chocolate and set the slice on the parchment-lined plate. Repeat with the remaining slice. Freeze the slices until the chocolate hardens, about 20 minutes. These can be made ahead, but remove them from the freezer about 5 minutes before serving.

Make the cocktails: Fill 2 old-fashioned glasses (or glasses of your choice) with ice and place in the freezer to chill. Make 1 cocktail at a time. In an ice-filled cocktail shaker, combine 4 ounces of orange juice, 2 ounces of mezcal, 6 shakes of Angostura bitters, and 4 shakes of chocolate bitters and shake vigorously for 15 seconds. Strain into a chilled glass. Make a ¼-inch cut into the undipped section of an orange slice and secure it to the rim of the glass (or float the orange slice on top of the cocktail). Repeat to make the second cocktail.

Bourbon Peach Smash

MAKES 2 COCKTAILS / TOTAL TIME: 5 MINUTES

1 very ripe peach

Ice

4 ounces bourbon

2 teaspoons brown sugar or honey

½ ounce fresh lemon juice

6 ounces ginger beer

Fresh basil or mint sprig, for garnish

I wanted a peach and bourbon drink for the book (because what an epic combination!), so I put on my lab coat and tried to science-up a peach-infused bourbon. But then I had to wait over a week for the flavors to come together and that was just too complicated, so I went a different route. Technically a smash is one of the earliest forms of cocktail; it's a type of julep with sugar, a liquor, and an herb (like mint) that gets "smashed." This cocktail kind of fits that description: The herb is basil, and I decided to smash the peaches to release all that gorgeous juicy flavor and give you a quick and easy cocktail that doesn't feel like a science experiment. Bourbon is a very rich spirit, so cutting it with ginger beer really balances it out, adding a nice bubbly spiciness and making it super drinkable.

Slice the peach into 8 slices, saving 2 slices for garnish. Add the remaining peach slices to a cocktail shaker and use a muddler or the end of a wooden spoon to muddle the peach. Add the ice, bourbon, brown sugar, and lemon juice and shake vigorously for 30 seconds. Strain into 2 ice-filled rocks glasses. Top off with ginger beer. Garnish each glass with a peach slice and fresh herb sprig.

Grilled Pineapple Spicy Margaritas

MAKES 2 COCKTAILS / TOTAL TIME: 15 MINUTES

½ cup fresh pineapple wedges or chunks

3 jalapeño slices (omit if you don't like spice)

Juice of 2 limes

4 ounces tequila, blanco or reposado, your preference

2 ounces Cointreau or other triple sec

2 ounces pineapple juice

1 ounce agave syrup

Ice

Fresh cilantro or mint sprig, for garnish

When you'd rather be lounging on a beach in Mexico (and honestly who wouldn't . . . always??), this margarita will get you there. And not to humble-brag, but I kind of outdid myself with this one. It was the first cocktail I made when I finished my outdoor kitchen and all of my friends freaked out over it. I knew right away that it had to go in the book! Bringing the grill into a glass is just such a delightful surprise and is a foolproof way to make sure everyone enjoys a cocktail or two while you grill up dinner. Muddle the jalapeño in the lime juice ahead of time for a little extra bite. If you have a muddler, use that, but a wooden spoon will do fine, too. I've even been known to use a rolling pin (girl's gotta do . . .)! Just text your friends to bring extra limes. I don't know why, but there are never enough limes. I tried to suggest one recipe here, but I couldn't decide because really, can't go wrong pairing this drink with pretty much any recipe in the book.

Preheat an outdoor grill or stovetop grill pan to high heat. Add the pineapple to the grill to slightly caramelize the sugars and create lovely grill marks, about 1 minute per side. Set aside 2 small chunks of pineapple for garnish.

Add the rest of the pineapple to a cocktail shaker. Add the jalapeño (if using) and lime juice and use a muddler or end of a wooden spoon to muddle everything together. Add the tequila, Cointreau, pineapple juice, agave syrup, and ice and shake vigorously. Strain into 2 ice-filled rocks glasses. Garnish with the reserved grilled pineapple and a sprig of cilantro or mint.

Blackberry Mexican Mule

MAKES 2 COCKTAILS / TOTAL TIME: 5 MINUTES

⅓ cup blackberries (about 2 ounces), plus more for garnish

4 fresh mint leaves, plus more for garnish

1 ounce lime juice

4 ounces tequila (I'm a Casamigos Blanco girl)

Ice

6 to 8 ounces ginger beer

Give me a big bowl of blackberries in the summertime and I am one happy gal. They are by far my favorite berries and inspired this juicy drink, but you could easily swap in any favorite berry. Although I love a traditional Moscow mule, served in that cool copper mug, I've taken this mule to Mexico by swapping out the vodka for my fave, tequila (duh), and added some plump blackberries to amp up the sexiness. If you have two copper mugs, go for it, but it's just as good in a rocks glass or even served in a big wineglass, like sangria. An added benefit, and why it's such a natural with big flavors and spicy food, is that the ginger beer excites your taste buds while it settles your stomach! It's great with Carnitas Taco Bar (page 152) or Dad's Oven-Baked Jammy Ribs (page 177).

In a cocktail shaker, combine the blackberries, mint, and lime juice and use a muddler or the end of a wooden spoon to muddle the mixture. Add the tequila and ice and shake. Strain into 2 ice-filled mule mugs or rocks glasses. Top off with the ginger beer, and garnish with blackberries and mint.

PIECE OF CAKE

Piece of cake. That's shorthand for something that's simple to do, but in fact most people think that the sweet thing that ends a meal is anything but simple. I'm here to flip that script so that dessert is a piece of cake, or easy as pie . . . or a bunch of other delicious treats that will have even the liars that "don't like sweets" grabbing seconds. Flourless Espresso Brownies (page 235), a simple Strawberry Skillet Galette (page 239), Pavlova (page 241), Spicy Fruit Salad (page 246), and yes, a Texas Sheet Cake (page 248), which I totally messed with by topping it with a nontraditional (but super-delish) Olive Oil Chocolate Frosting. What's extra sweet about these recipes are the little tweaks and twists

I've included, like the pretzel crust for the No-Bake Key Lime Pie (page 236), or the fact that you can throw together the Salty, Crunchy Fudge (page 245) in under an hour with common pantry ingredients. For the slightly more involved recipes, I'm with you every step of the way—I'm the first to admit that I'm not an expert baker, so I tested and tested and rewrote and reworked these recipes so they would be clear and really easy to follow. Like a piece of really decadent cake.

Flourless Espresso Brownies

SERVES 6 / TOTAL TIME: 30 MINUTES

Softened unsalted butter or cooking spray for the pan

2 cups chocolate chips or 12 ounces chopped chocolate

1⅓ sticks (10½ tablespoons) unsalted butter

4 large eggs

1 cup sugar

¼ cup cacao powder

1 heaping teaspoon espresso powder (see Note)

¼ cup tapioca starch or cornstarch

Flaky sea salt, for garnish

This recipe brings together what might possibly be the two strongest flavor fan bases: chocolate lovers and coffee lovers. My allegiance to both is unwavering and when I decided to master a flourless brownie recipe, it felt like a disservice to not add espresso. The espresso powder gives these decadent, fudgy brownies another layer of richness and flavor. You can also whip these up in one bowl (which I clean while they bake) for a simple process and easy cleanup. I love randomly whipping these up after having dinner with friends. No one ever turns them down!

Espresso powder is different from just ground espresso beans and can usually be found in the baking section of most stores. One jar does last a long time, though! If you're not feeling the coffee flavor or if you just don't want to buy an ingredient for just one recipe, you can totally leave it out and enjoy the brownies in their pure, chocolatey form. They're still amazing!

NOTE

Feel free to add another teaspoon or 2 of espresso powder for extra coffee flavor, or omit it altogether if it isn't your thing. They'll still turn out great without it!

Preheat the oven to 350°F. Grease an 8-inch square baking pan with the butter.

In a microwave-safe bowl, combine the chocolate chips and butter and microwave at 50 percent (chocolate burns very easily, so this is important!) in 30-second increments, stirring after each, until melted, 2 to 3 minutes. (Alternatively, melt the chocolate and butter in a heatproof bowl set over a pan of simmering water on low heat. Do not let the bowl touch the water.) Let the chocolate mixture cool slightly.

In a large bowl, whisk together the eggs and sugar and set aside.

In a medium bowl, whisk together the cacao powder, espresso powder, and

tapioca starch to combine, making sure there are no lumps.

Make sure the melted chocolate mixture is slightly cool before adding to the egg mixture. Whisk the melted chocolate into the egg mixture until the batter is smooth. Using a rubber spatula, gently fold in the cacao mixture. Pour the batter into the prepared pan.

Bake until a toothpick inserted in the center comes out clean, 25 to 30 minutes; you're better off underbaking than overbaking these!

Garnish with lots of flaky sea salt before cutting into squares and serving.

No-Bake Key Lime Pie with Pretzel Crust

SERVES 6 / TOTAL TIME: 25 MINUTES, PLUS 3 HOURS OR OVERNIGHT FOR CHILLING

PRETZEL CRUST

Softened unsalted butter or cooking spray for the pie plate

1½ cups pretzel crumbs, medium (from about 3 cups whole pretzels)

1½ sticks (12 tablespoons) unsalted butter, melted

¼ cup packed light brown sugar

¼ teaspoon kosher salt

FILLING

1 (14-ounce) can sweetened condensed milk

8 ounces cream cheese, at room temperature

1 cup key lime juice

Grated zest of 2 limes, plus more for garnish

2 cups heavy whipping cream, divided

2 tablespoons powdered sugar

I was so lucky to try key lime pie for the first time in none other than Key West, where this iconic dessert originated. So my love affair began at an early age on a family trip to Florida, where my dad grew up, and when I came back to California I had trouble meeting my very high standards for what key lime pie should taste like. Although this recipe may not be traditional (my dad almost took me out of his will when I made him a key lime pie without the graham cracker crust), it still embodies everything that this delicious dessert should be: crunchy, creamy, silky, sweet, tart, and a bit salty. This pie takes only about 25 minutes to throw together (and then just a couple of hours for it to chill), plus it's a no-bake recipe! Once you master the pretzel crust, you'll be using it for everything from chocolate custard pie to an ice cream topping. Size matters here, so make sure you get medium or thick pretzels—it really makes a difference to the crunchy crust. As for the key lime juice, you can use Nellie & Joe's bottled juice, but freshly squeezed regular limes or even lemons will not disappoint. (You could even use fresh key limes, but keep in mind they are so small it takes forever to get the amount of juice needed.) If you do opt for fresh regular limes, remember that key lime juice is tarter, so you might need a bit more juice to balance against the sugar.

Grease a 9-inch pie plate with the butter.

Make the pretzel crust: In a food processor, pulse the pretzels for about 10 seconds, until they are medium crushed, taking care not to pulse to a fine powder. Add the melted butter, brown sugar, and salt and pulse about 5 times until the butter is evenly incorporated, the pretzels are a medium-fine crumb, and the mixture holds together when squeezed in your hand.

Transfer the pretzel mixture to the pie plate and use a glass or measuring cup to press the dough evenly into the bottom of the pie plate and up the sides. You can use your hands for this if you prefer. This can be made ahead if wrapped tightly and refrigerated for up to 3 days or frozen.

Make the filling: In a stand mixer (or in a bowl with a handheld mixer), combine the condensed milk, cream cheese, lime zest, and lime juice and beat on medium speed until smooth, 1 to 2 minutes, and set aside.

In a separate bowl, whip 1 cup of the heavy cream and 1 tablespoon of the powdered sugar until firm peaks are formed.

236 / Seriously, So Good

With a rubber spatula, gently fold the whipped cream into the cream cheese mixture, taking care not to deflate the cream. Using the spatula, fill the pie crust and smooth the top, then cover the pie with plastic wrap.

Chill in the fridge for at least 3 hours or overnight.

Before serving, whip the remaining 1 cup of the heavy whipping cream and 1 tablespoon of the powdered sugar to stiff peaks and cover the pie with the cream. Top the whipped cream with grated lime zest and serve! Keep any leftovers covered and refrigerated for up to 3 days.

Strawberry Skillet Galette

SERVES 6 / TOTAL TIME: 1½ HOURS, PLUS CHILLING AND SETTING TIME

1½ cups all-purpose flour

2 tablespoons sugar

½ teaspoon kosher salt

1 stick (8 tablespoons) plus 2 tablespoons very cold or frozen unsalted butter, cut into 24 pieces

¼ cup ice water

FRUIT FILLING

2½ pounds strawberries, sliced (about 5 cups)

¾ cup sugar

1 tablespoon cornstarch or tapioca starch

Grated zest and juice of 1 small lemon

¼ teaspoon kosher salt

ASSEMBLY

2 tablespoons unsalted butter, cut into small pieces

1 large egg yolk, beaten

Raw sugar, for sprinkling

NOTE

I buy precut parchment paper sheets the size of a half-sheet pan (13 x 18 inches) in bulk from King Arthur Baking. They make rolling out the dough very easy. You just slip the dough on the parchment right into the pan!

I love a good old American apple pie, but this take on the classic is a cooler, chicer French version that is ten times easier to make and way more delicious. Sorry, I know that sounds sacrilegious but if apple pie is dinner at Applebee's, this galette is medium-rare steak with a dry martini. Don't get me wrong, I like riblets as much as the next girl, but I'll opt for the bustling bistro every time. "Galette" is a fancy French word for a free-form tart, and this recipe is an all-star because the dough is super versatile and can be used for any of your favorite pies. You can even omit the sugar and use it for a savory pie (sautéed veggies with bacon and cheese, anyone?). Though lots of galettes are baked free-form, with the dough just plopped on a sheet pan, the cast-iron skillet makes things so much easier, since the yummy juices stay inside the tart and nothing spills over to burn on your oven floor. Swap the berries for the fruit of your choice; just make sure to taste the filling and adjust the amount of sugar depending on how sweet or acidic the swap is. Don't be intimidated! Once you master this, you're practically a pastry chef!

Make the galette dough: In a food processor, combine the flour, sugar, and salt and pulse a few times to blend. Distribute the butter over the flour mixture and pulse 8 to 10 times until the mixture looks like coarse cornmeal. Slowly begin to add the ice water and pulse, continuing to add the water and pulsing until the water has been incorporated.

Scrape the sides and bottom of the bowl if the dough is sticking and continue to pulse until you have a dough that forms small lumps that hold together when you gently press them. It's very important to not let the dough completely come together or become a ball or you will have a tough dough. Turn the dough out onto a clean counter.

Gently use the heel of your hand to push all of the dough away from you across the counter to blend the butter into the flour and then gather all of the dough into a ball, flatten it into a disk about 6 inches wide, and wrap it tightly in plastic wrap. Refrigerate the dough for 30 minutes. (Well wrapped, the dough can be refrigerated for up to 2 days or frozen for up to 2 months.)

Remove the dough from the fridge and let it sit for 5 to 10 minutes. You'll know it's ready when you press it shouldn't begin to crack.

Place the dough between 2 large pieces of parchment paper (see Note) and roll the dough into a round, about 12 inches in diameter. It doesn't have to be the exact size or have perfect edges—remember this is a rustic dessert!

Transfer the dough without removing the bottom layer of parchment to a 10- or 10½-inch cast-iron or ovenproof skillet and gently press the dough into the bottom of the pan. Chill in the refrigerator while you prepare the filling.

Preheat the oven to 400°F.

About 10 minutes before you are ready to bake, remove the dough from the refrigerator.

Make the fruit filling: In a large bowl, combine the strawberries, sugar, 3 teaspoons of the cornstarch, the lemon zest, lemon juice, and salt and mix to evenly combine. Let the fruit sit for about 10 minutes. If there is more than a ¼ cup of liquid after you add the sugar, add more cornstarch, a teaspoon at a time, so the liquid has a sauce-like consistency.

Assemble the galette: Pour the fruit mixture into the skillet and gently pleat or fold the edges of the dough around the fruit. If the dough is too cold to fold without cracking, let it sit out for another few minutes. Top the fruit with the bits of butter. Brush the dough with the egg yolk and sprinkle with the raw sugar.

Bake until the fruit is bubbling and the crust is golden, 50 minutes to 1 hour. If the fruit or the crust is becoming too dark, cover the area with foil for the remainder of the baking time.

Set the skillet on a cooling rack and let it rest for 20 minutes so that the juices thicken. You can serve straight from the pan with ice cream or whipped cream, or carefully loosen the bottom of the galette with a spatula, lift the parchment, and transfer to a serving platter (removing the paper).

Pavlova

SERVES 6 / TOTAL TIME: 1½ HOURS, PLUS COOLING TIME, ABOUT 1 ADDITIONAL HOUR

6 large egg whites

1¼ cups sugar

1 teaspoon distilled white vinegar

½ teaspoon vanilla extract

2 teaspoons cornstarch

1½ cups heavy cream

2 cups mixed berries

Fresh mint sprigs, for garnish

Pavlova is a meringue cake topped with whipped cream and fresh fruit that is basically like eating a sugary cloud. There's no reason to be intimidated by this elegant dessert once you get the egg whites whipping technique down. This is one of those recipes that reads way more complicated than it is, I promise! Meringues are also really versatile: You can add cocoa powder and chocolate, espresso powder, or even mini chocolate chips, or make individual pavlovas with the same baking time. It's also a fantastic gluten-free dessert, and makes an excellent birthday cake. A few tips: Make sure there is no fat in the bowl or on the whisk you're using to beat the egg whites—fat is the enemy when you are whipping egg whites. I wipe the bowl and whisk with a wet paper towel dabbed with white vinegar for good luck! Also, I suggest not making these on a humid day. Humidity will make the meringue weep liquid, and you'll be left with messy meringues.

Preheat the oven to 350°F.

Lightly trace an 8-inch round or oval (your preference, I usually match the shape to the serving dish) on a sheet of parchment paper. Flip the parchment over (so the meringue is not piped over the pencil tracing) and place on a sheet pan.

In a stand mixer fitted with the whisk (or in a bowl with a handheld mixer), beat the egg whites on medium-high speed until soft peaks form, about 5 minutes. Slowly add the sugar while beating, a few spoonfuls at a time, and when all of the sugar is added, increase the speed to high and continue beating until the meringue is stiff and glossy. (You should, as Julia Child did, be able to hold the meringue over your head without it falling out, but I don't advise!) Add the vinegar and vanilla and beat until evenly incorporated.

If using a stand mixer, remove the bowl from the base. Using a small sieve, sift the cornstarch over the meringue, and gently fold the cornstarch into the meringue, taking care not to deflate the eggs.

With the spatula, spread the meringue into a solid round using the tracing as a guide. You can use the back of a spoon to make decorative peaks around the edges, although do not make them too high or spiky, as they may burn. Gently press down the center of the meringue to make a small nest for the whipped cream and berries that will fill it later.

Reduce the oven temperature to 250°F. Bake the meringue for 1 hour 15 minutes. Turn off the oven, open the oven door, and allow the meringue to cool in the oven. The meringue should feel firm outside and slightly soft inside and will be a pale ivory in color. Once cool, about another hour, using a spatula, carefully transfer the meringue to a cooling rack.

In a stand mixer fitted with the whisk (or in a bowl with a handheld mixer), whip the heavy cream on high speed until soft peaks form, 2 to 3 minutes. Spread in the center of the meringue, top with berries, and garnish with mint sprigs.

CHOCOLATE PAVLOVA VARIATION:

When making the meringue, sift in ¼ cup cocoa powder along with the cornstarch. Gently fold ¼ cup finely chopped bittersweet or semisweet chocolate into the meringue, spread on the parchment paper, and continue as directed.

Salty, Crunchy Fudge

SERVES 6 / TOTAL TIME: 10 MINUTES, PLUS 1 HOUR FOR CHILLING

Softened unsalted butter or cooking spray for the pan

2½ cups semisweet chocolate chips

1 (14-ounce) can sweetened condensed milk

1 teaspoon vanilla extract

½ teaspoon kosher salt

1½ cups crushed potato chips (about 5 cups whole potato chips)

2 cups crushed pretzels

1 teaspoon flaky sea salt

1 teaspoon raw sugar

Rainy days. A movie. Celebrating. Crying. Summertime. Festive holiday feels. You name it. This is a delicious and dynamic dessert recipe for those or any other occasion, and it only takes ten minutes to throw together. Definitely my vibe! Take liberties with the potato chips, as I know everyone has different favorites. Sometimes I like Cape Cod waffle-cut chips for the extra crunch, but these are just as wonderful with the regular salted variety. Once you've mastered this recipe, there are endless ways to play with it to make it your own. Add chile for some heat, mix in your favorite nut or sweetened coconut flakes, even swirl in some peanut butter! You can go boozy with a bourbon-and-pecan variety, or holiday themed (with white chocolate, cracked peppermint candies, or candy corn for Halloween), or add espresso powder and chocolate-covered espresso beans with a shot of Baileys for a late-night treat. It's no-fail fun!

Lightly grease an 8-inch square baking pan with the butter. Cut 2 pieces of parchment paper the width of the pan and long enough to come an inch or so above 2 sides of the pan. Place the pieces crisscross to one another so parchment is sticking up on all 4 sides. These will help you remove the fudge.

In a large microwave-safe bowl, combine the chocolate chips and condensed milk and microwave in 30-second increments, stirring after each, until the chocolate is melted, about 1 minute. (Alternatively, melt the chocolate and sweetened condensed milk in a heatproof bowl set over a pan of simmering water over low heat. Do not let the bowl touch the water.)

Add the vanilla and salt to the chocolate mixture and use a spatula to combine. Gently stir in the potato chips and transfer to the prepared pan. Smooth the top of the fudge and gently press the pretzels on top of the fudge. Sprinkle with the flaky sea salt and raw sugar and refrigerate for 1 hour.

Using the handles, remove the fudge from the pan. Using a sharp knife, cut the fudge into triangles or squares, small or large, the size is up to you! Serve immediately or store in an airtight container, unrefrigerated, for up to 1 week.

Spicy Fruit Salad

SERVES 4 / TOTAL TIME: 10 MINUTES

5 to 6 cups bite-size pieces mixed fruit, such as watermelon, mango, pineapple, strawberries, honeydew, cucumber, and jicama

Juice of 2 limes

2 tablespoons finely chopped fresh mint leaves

1 tablespoon Tajín (or 1 tablespoon chili powder and 1 teaspoon kosher salt)

Fresh mint sprigs, for garnish

I felt it was my job to make fruit salad hip again, and I'm pretty sure I nailed it with this one. It's extremely refreshing, but packs a nice little punch from Tajín, the citrusy, mildly spicy Mexican seasoning blend of chiles, lime, and salt. Spending time in Mexico really hooked me on Tajín and the nice zing it gives fresh fruit. It's usually sprinkled on top when you buy cut fruit from a street vendor down there, and really accentuates the natural sweetness of anything. It's also delicious on vegetables like carrots and cucumbers. You can really use any fruit you like in this, but I highly suggest watermelon, mango, and pineapple, as they pair really well with the Tajín. Jicama is also a super-fun addition. It's a root vegetable that has the crisp texture of an apple but really doesn't have much sweetness. It's a nice counterbalance to any sweet fruit you use and adds a fun texture! I like to serve these in pretty individual cups instead of one big bowl. Try it out.

NOTE

This can be made 1 hour in advance, covered and refrigerated.

In a large bowl, combine the fruit, lime juice, mint, and Tajín and gently toss to combine evenly. Garnish with fresh mint sprigs.

Texas Sheet Cake with Olive Oil Chocolate Frosting

SERVES 10 TO 12 / TOTAL TIME: 35 MINUTES

CAKE

Softened butter for the pan

2 large eggs

½ cup buttermilk or sour cream

1½ teaspoons vanilla extract

2 cups all-purpose flour

2 cups sugar

1 teaspoon baking soda

½ teaspoon kosher salt

2 sticks (16 tablespoons) unsalted butter, at room temperature

⅓ cup unsweetened cocoa powder

1 cup boiling water

FROSTING

4 cups powdered sugar

¾ cup unsweetened cocoa powder or cacao powder

¼ teaspoon kosher salt

¾ to 1 cup extra-virgin olive oil

¾ cup half-and-half, warmed

1 teaspoon vanilla extract

NOTE

Store tightly wrapped at room temperature for up to 2 days, or in the fridge for 1 week. You can also freeze it for up to 3 months.

You're not supposed to mess with Texas, but I'm taking a few liberties with the state's famed cake because my favorite is from Yellow Rose, a café in NYC's East Village. Those New Yorkers sneak extra-virgin olive oil into the chocolate frosting and I personally think it's just the tweak this decadent chocolate cake needs. Look for a less peppery, more floral olive oil. If you're into the more traditional Texas way, feel free to toast a cup of chopped pecans and add them to your frosting. If you're feeling adventurous or celebrating the coffee lover in your life, swap in a cup of hot coffee for the boiling water in the batter, for a more intensely flavored treat that cuts down on the sweetness just the right amount. You can also add a bit of chili powder to the frosting for a sly punch. It's important to make the frosting and spread it over the cake while warm for that beautiful smooth finish. If you're intimidated by baking a cake from scratch, don't be. It's really not much more complicated than the boxed stuff. Just give it a shot once and I promise you'll do it yourself from then on. I don't consider myself the best baker by any means, but my dad *still* raves about this being the best cake he's ever had! I guess I know what he's getting for his birthday every year.

Make the cake: Preheat the oven to 350°F. Butter or line with parchment a 13 x 18-inch sheet pan.

In a medium bowl, whisk the eggs, buttermilk, and vanilla and set aside. In a large bowl, whisk together the flour, sugar, baking soda, and salt.

In a medium saucepan, melt the butter over medium heat and add the cocoa powder, stirring frequently. Add the boiling water and stir constantly for 30 seconds.

Make a well in the center of the dry ingredients, pour the cocoa mixture into the center well, and, using a spatula, gently fold until no flour remains. Gently fold in the buttermilk mixture.

Pour the batter into the prepared pan, spreading evenly. Bake until a toothpick inserted into the center comes out with a few crumbs clinging (you don't want to have the cake be too dry), 18 to 20 minutes. Set the pan on a wire rack to cool.

Make the frosting: In a large bowl, sift the powdered sugar and cocoa powder together. Whisk in the salt.

While whisking continuously, drizzle in the olive oil and half-and-half, alternating them, until you have a glossy frosting. Whisk in the vanilla extract.

Smooth the frosting on while the cake is still warm. Allow the cake to cool completely, and cut into squares to serve.

Oatmeal Cookie Pies

MAKES 6 COOKIE PIES / TOTAL TIME: 30 MINUTES

OATMEAL COOKIES

1¼ cups all-purpose flour

½ teaspoon baking powder

½ teaspoon salt

1½ cups rolled oats (not quick-cooking)

1 stick (8 tablespoons) unsalted butter, at room temperature

⅔ cup coconut sugar or light brown sugar

⅓ cup granulated sugar

1 large egg

2 teaspoons pure vanilla extract

Flaky sea salt, optional

CREAM CHEESE FROSTING

8 ounces cream cheese, at room temperature

1 stick (4 ounces) unsalted butter, at room temperature

1 teaspoon vanilla extract

Pinch of kosher salt

3½ cups powdered sugar

I created this recipe for someone I love very dearly whose favorite dessert is an oatmeal cookie pie—a nostalgic classic that's super fun to make (and also very kid friendly!). I make the cookies for my oatmeal cookie pies a bit larger than a normal cookie, but this recipe totally works if you want to make the standard, smaller variety (don't forget to add chocolate or butterscotch chips, if that's how you roll). The cream cheese frosting is good enough to eat out of the bowl and will become a staple for countless baked goods, from banana bread to cupcakes. I also love making just the oatmeal cookies for a weekend treat with my morning coffee. Yum!

Preheat the oven to 375°F. Line 2 sheet pans with parchment paper.

Make the oatmeal cookies: In a medium bowl, whisk together the flour, baking powder, and salt. Stir in the oats and set aside.

In a stand mixer fitted with the paddle (or in a bowl with a handheld mixer), beat the butter and both sugars on medium-high speed until light and fluffy, 2 to 3 minutes. Scrape down the sides with a rubber spatula. Reduce the speed to low and beat in the egg and vanilla until well mixed, about 1 minute. Slowly add the oat/flour mixture in batches, taking care not to overmix.

Use a ¼-cup measure to drop balls of dough about 2 inches apart on the lined sheet pans. If desired, sprinkle with flaky sea salt. Bake until cookies are golden around the edges, but still soft in the center, 11 to 14 minutes.

Remove from the oven and let cool on the sheet pans for 1 to 2 minutes. Transfer to a wire rack to cool completely while you make the frosting.

Make the cream cheese frosting: In a stand mixer fitted with the whisk (or in a bowl with a handheld mixer), beat the cream cheese and butter on high speed until smooth, about 1 minute. Beat in the vanilla and salt. Reduce the speed to medium and slowly add the powdered sugar, beating until the frosting is thick and spreadable.

Using an offset spatula or a table knife, spread about 3 generous tablespoons of frosting on the flat side of the cooled cookie. Gently press together to form a sandwich/pie.

Rosemary Almond Orange Olive Oil Cake

SERVES 6 TO 8 / TOTAL TIME: 1 HOUR 15 MINUTES

CAKE

Extra-virgin olive oil for the pan

1¾ cups sugar

1½ tablespoons grated orange zest

1 tablespoon chopped fresh rosemary

1½ cups all-purpose flour

½ cup almond flour

1½ teaspoons kosher salt

½ teaspoon baking soda

½ teaspoon baking powder

3 large eggs

1¼ cups whole milk

⅓ cup extra-virgin olive oil

¼ cup Grand Marnier

¼ cup freshly squeezed orange juice

ICING

¾ cup powdered sugar

3 tablespoons freshly squeezed orange juice, or more as needed

GARNISH

1 pint raspberries

Fresh rosemary sprigs

There's something so classy about olive oil cake—it's fancy yet simple and *always* a crowd-pleaser. This version, framed after the dessert at the Italian trattoria Maialino in NYC, adds just a few extra ingredients to really step it up from the average. Olive oil replaces the usual butter, but I use a light-tasting extra-virgin olive oil that isn't aggressively peppery. Pulsing the sugar with the rosemary and orange zest helps release the oils and perfume the sugar for more flavor. And the cake is versatile. It can be made entirely with all-purpose flour, or you can substitute cornmeal or whole wheat flour for the almond flour. Almost any spirit works, too; try amaretto or brandy or kirsch. There are tons of liberties to be taken to suit your needs! The cake rises quite a bit while baking so make sure your cake pan is at least 2 inches deep. And if you're not an icing person (can't relate), you can serve it with whipped cream, ice cream, or even sorbet!

Make the cake: Preheat the oven to 350°F. Oil a 9-inch round cake pan that is at least 2 inches deep and line the bottom with a round of parchment paper.

In a small food processor, combine the sugar, orange zest, and chopped rosemary and pulse for 10 to 20 seconds to combine.

Transfer the sugar mixture to a medium bowl. Whisk in both flours, the salt, baking soda, and baking powder. In a large bowl, whisk together the eggs, milk, olive oil, Grand Marnier, and orange juice. Add the flour mixture to the wet ingredients and whisk until just combined.

Pour the batter into the prepared pan, place on a sheet pan, and bake until

the top is golden and a toothpick inserted in the center comes out clean, 50 to 60 minutes.

Let the cake cool in the pan on a rack for 30 minutes.

Run a knife around the edge of the pan, invert the cake onto the rack, turn right side up, and let cool.

Make the icing: Add the powdered sugar to a small bowl. Slowly whisk enough orange juice until you have a pourable icing.

Garnish: Set the cake on a rack set over a piece of parchment or foil. Drizzle the icing over the cake. Top with the raspberries and fresh rosemary sprigs.

Bananas Foster

SERVES 4 / TOTAL TIME: 15 MINUTES

1 pint vanilla ice cream

¾ cup packed coconut sugar or light brown sugar

½ stick (4 tablespoons) unsalted butter

2 tablespoons coconut oil

½ teaspoon ground cinnamon

2 ripe bananas, halved lengthwise

⅓ cup banana liqueur

½ cup dark rum

Bananas Foster holds a special place in my heart because it was one of the first desserts I ever learned how to make. I remember trying it in my parents' kitchen and being shocked at how delicious it was—and I've been hooked ever since. I keep this New Orleans dessert in my arsenal because: It doesn't take me away from my guests, I get to put on a show, and there's no extra shopping. If this is your kind of dessert, spend a little extra on the banana liqueur; look for it online. A good brand for all sorts of liqueurs is Giffard. But if you really don't want to buy yet another liqueur, just add more rum in place of the banana liqueur. Using coconut sugar instead of the usual brown sugar and adding some coconut oil with the butter ups the flavor, too. If twelve-year-old me can make it, so can you!

Using a ½-cup ice cream scoop, scoop the ice cream into 8 balls onto a plate and place in the freezer. Cover if not using right away.

In a large skillet, combine the sugar, butter, coconut oil, and cinnamon over medium heat and stir until the butter melts, about 2 minutes. Add the banana halves, banana liqueur, and rum and cook until the bananas have softened, stirring the sugar mixture and gently turning and basting the bananas occasionally, about 3 minutes.

Remove the pan from the heat and away from any flammable objects, then use a long kitchen match or igniter to ignite the alcohol and gently shake the pan until the flame dies, about 30 seconds.

Place 2 scoops of ice cream on each dish and top each dish with 2 banana halves and evenly distribute the sauce. Serve immediately.

Index